NETWORKING FAMILIES IN CRISIS

Intervention Strategies with Families and Social Networks

Uri Rueveni, Ph.D.

Eastern Pennsylvania Psychiatric Institute
Philadelphia Pennsylvania

 **HUMAN SCIENCES PRESS**
72 Fifth Avenue   3 Henrietta Street
NEW YORK, NY 10011 ● LONDON, WC2E 8LU

Library of Congress Catalog Number 78-8024

ISBN: 0-87705-374-x

Copyright © 1979 by Human Sciences Press
72 Fifth Avenue, New York, New York 10011

Printed in the United States of America
9 987654321

Library of Congress Cataloging in Publication Data

Rueveni, Uri
   Networking families in crisis.

   Includes bibliographical references and index.
   1. Family psychotherapy. 2. Crisis intervention
(Psychiatry) I. Title.
RC488.5.R83   616.8'915   78-8024
ISBN 0-87705-374-X

To my family network
and to the network of friends who
helped many families to get in touch.

PREFACE

We live in an age of increasing exploration of inner and outer space. In the psychological realm, increasing turmoil and polemic swirls over the choice of individual versus group methods to treat the troubled person. Depth psychology, as elaborated in the schools of Freud, Jung, and Adler to Fromm, Horney, and Sullivan, still champions the individual psychotherapy approach. This works for many people, particularly the better educated, more affluent, and less severely incapacitated. Group methods are usually employed after individual therapy attempts have faltered or when social disability or deviance is present.

Since the 1950s, increasing attention has been given to the family (those persons living in the same home) as the primary locus of psychopathology. The problem and the solution is seen to be in the family system. Concepts such as scapegoating, double binds, mystification, symbiosis, sick role reinforcement, and family collusions and secrets attest to an external, interpersonal view of psychopathology.

The social network intervention method (called "networking" in this book) is in our opinion a logical extension of the family systems rationale. It evolved from working with individuals and families in which the crises were too great, too overwhelming, or where too many extended family members or significant others produced a stalemate in attempts to change an unlivable situation.

Our work has confirmed the earlier findings of anthropologists (e.g., Barnes and Bott) that family functioning is influenced greatly by, and is often interwoven with its surrounding social network of kin, friends, neighbors, intimates, social groups, and those who perform personal services. We are beginning to see a vicious circle/cycle that is producing emotional distress and illness.

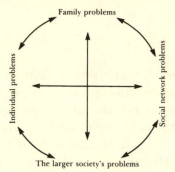

The need for human support systems is a historically demonstrated necessity from the hunting and gathering societies through the current stopgap measures such as crisis intervention, hot lines, and growth centers. In industrial society there has been a loss of effective extended family and network support. Through these natural systems one finds jobs, help, friends, companionship, and social relations that make life worth living.

However, there are counterforces, left and right. Some professionals feel that secret-breaking violates the confidential relationship. Others feel that secrecy is the basis of power. So everyone is defined, confined within a certain legal limit. Secrecy is distinct from confidentiality. It has a quality of collusiveness and power over someone. Confidentiality is usually only possible in a twosome relationship —doctor and patient, lawyer and client, priest and confessioner. Related concepts are privacy and intimacy. The intimacy of the bedroom may be private, but it is not secret (unless used as a weaponry system). There is the implication that one or more persons know something that others do not know and therefore the latter is powerless. Secrecy can be beneficent or maleficent. Santa Claus is an example of the former, and the boogyman is an example of the latter. Malfunctioning systems rely heavily on secrecy. A central concept of network intervention is the demystification of secrets; this allows the system to change.

Dr. Rueveni's book clearly shows the technique and theory he uses in extending the boundaries of professional intervention in families in severe crisis by utilizing the natural resources within an individual's network and the larger culture.

This book should be read by professional workers in the field of crisis intervention, and also by persons with problems who might need the help of their network. Finally, it is a book of great importance to all of us, professional or patient. It is of utmost importance to those of us who comprise the network.

We have to confess a certain prejudice-bias in talking about this book. Uri and his wife Mira are friends and co-workers. We think that everyone needs a tribe, a clan, a group, a family, an extended family, a family of families, a Karrass, a network, a Saturday night pub, a trip, a dream, a world.

Ross V. Speck
Joan L. Speck

Philadelphia, Pennsylvania
1978

CONTENTS

INTRODUCTION

The family system is an important source of emotional support for most of us. When family members experience emotional stress and their relationships reach a crisis point, support for change and for a productive resolution of the crisis can often come from the extended system of family, relatives, and friends. Mobilizing the social network for help and support during a difficult family crisis usually results in constructive changes that lead toward a resolution of the immediate family crisis.

Speck and Attneave (1973) describe the social network intervention process as follows: "Forces of healing are set up within the living social fabric of people whose distress led society and the members to label their behavior pathological." They further argue that "the energies and talents of people can be focused to provide the essential supports, satisfactions and controls for one another, and that these potentials are present in the social network of family, neighbors, friends, and associates of the person or family in distress."

When the family network is mobilized effectively, communicating among members improves and tensions are reduced; relationships among family members can become more intimate, caring, and supportive. A sense of greater involvement and commitment for help develops between the family and other members of its social network.

Family network intervention is not a substitute for other forms of therapeutic interventions. It provides effective resolution of difficult and often desperate family crises. The networking process tries to change the existing malfunctioning and potentially destructive patterns of family relationships. It can strengthen the family by providing support for the development of alternative options in solving a crisis.

This book is written primarily for the professional who works with families and who would like to help the family reconnect with its larger social network. The focus is on shifting more responsibility for family healing and change from tranquilizers and hospitals to the family and its natural social network support system of relatives, friends, and neighbors. The book will familiarize professionals working in the mental health field with the processes and techniques of helping families in crisis to assemble and mobilize the extended system. The material is based on personal clinical experiences and those of other team members in our efforts to help families in emotional crisis reconnect with their family, friends, and others in the social support system. Mobilizing the social support system often requires an ongoing commitment to the concept that crisis resolution, healing, and constructive changes in our lives occur when relationships to our family and friends can be based on mutual trust, interconnectedness, and support. A few words on the use of the term "therapist" and the therapist's role with extended social systems are necessary. I chose to use the term therapist because I believe that therapists can and do have to become involved more intensely with larger social systems. Throughout this book I have used the terms, intervener, convener, network intervention, and network leader, terms that, in my judgment, describe the roles of the therapist when working with large support systems.

The first chapter in this book cites some studies that relate to issues of social support and the usefulness of operating within such a framework. No attempt is made here at a critical review of these studies, and no claim is made that all relevant studies on networks have been reviewed.

The second chapter introduces the concept and process of family network intervention—a process that includes at least one "screening" meeting with the nuclear family at home or in a mutually convenient location, the description of the intervention process with its unfolding six network phases, and a discussion of the criteria used for selecting a family for this modality of intervention and the important roles of the temporary support structures that follow the intervention process. This chapter also includes brief vignettes of four family dysfunctions leading toward crises that were dealt with by mobilizing the extended family and friendship support systems.

Four additional family network interventions are described in Chapter 3. The first is an attempt to help a drug-abusing family member stop her self-destructive acts and find resources within the network that could be helpful in her attempt to change.

The second family assembled its extended support system to help a mother, her ex-husband, their 14-year-old, so labeled "psychotic" daughter, and their five children, ranging in age from 9 to 17 years, to change their dysfunctional and crisis-oriented pattern of relationships.

The third family network intervention describes efforts made to help a mother and her two grown daughters who live with her to assemble a network of friends and friends of friends in order to help them separate and possibly change their ongoing crisis.

The fourth case describes the potential usefulness of utilizing the network support system to help a therapist and her patient discontinue a self-destructive relationship.

The goals of intervention and the roles undertaken by the network team are presented in Chapter 4.

Referral, confidentiality, videotaping, team development, and leadership issues are discussed in Chapter 5.

Training the professional to work with extended systems is described in Chapter 6. Chapter 7 provides some of the techniques available for networking families in crisis. A transcription of a first network intervention meeting is given in Chapter 8. Professionals working in a variety of settings may have to modify and adapt the use of the networking process. Chapter 9 describes several uses and adaptations of utilizing the social support system in hospitals, community, and school settings.

Many people were helpful to me prior to and during the process of writing this book. Ross and Joan Speck, my good friends and mentors, continually encouraged me in my efforts to complete the book; from them I have learned much about working with families. Members of my first network intervention team, Muriel Wiener, Miriam Shore, Robert Carroll, S. J. Marks, and Leslie Daroff, participated effectively in many networks. Members of my advance family network seminar, Alex Scott, C. Aquirre, Edgar Wiggins. Carmella Koussis, Ellen Lynch, Richard Rapoport, and Phillip Miraglia all were involved in intensive discussions and helpful exchanges. To my colleagues Marvin Greenberg, Loren Crabtree, Gerald Zuk, and Lydia Schut. John Frikor helped in videotaping a number of network sessions, and Marvin Fisher edited the videotapes. Jean Leech Johnson typed the manuscripts. And, finally, I thank my two children, Roni and Deena, and my wife, Mira, a family therapist who initiated and developed a network of parents in school.

Chapter 1

SOCIAL NETWORKS AS A SUPPORT SYSTEM

The dictionary defines "network" as any pattern or system that interconnects, a linking device, a communication system, a supporting device. The term network has been in use increasingly in the fields of anthropology, psychology, communications, geography, sociology, and related disciplines. Basically, it conveys interdependence, flow, linkage, interactions, and meshing of structures—a system. One definition of our social network is that it consists of that group of people who maintain an important, often ongoing, relationship in our lives. These people could be family, relatives, friends, neighbors, or other individuals in the community within which we interact.

Effective intervention efforts at healing emotional crises of individuals and families need to be linked to a larger community of social support systems. There are increasing indications as to the importance of the social support structure in our daily life, particularly during crisis periods. Studies indicate that effective crisis resolution depends on mobilization of community resources and support systems. Some of these studies deal with crisis intervention with suicidal patients (Selkin & Braucht, 1976), hospital settings (Foxman, 1976; Hansell, 1967; Langsley & Yarvis, 1976), community crisis (Brown, 1976), and natural disasters (McGree & Heffron, 1976; Kliman, 1976; Cohen, 1976).

We function within numerous interdependent social network support systems, some of which are our own family, friendships, neighborhood, work, professional, religious, and civic networks. When a crisis occurs in our life, especially an emotional crisis, effective mobilization of these supportive networks could be helpful in crisis resolution.

In an attempt to identify and explore the structural components of networks, Boissevain (1974) describes five concentric network zones: one personal, two intimate, one effective, and one nominal. The personal network zone includes close relatives and intimate friends. The first intimate zone includes close relatives and friends with whom one keeps active contacts, while the second intimate zone includes friends and relatives with whom one does not maintain frequent contacts. The effective zone consists of people who are not emotionally involved with the individual, but who have economic and political relationships. The nominal zone consists of people who have little or no relationship or contact to one's own self. Boissevain further states that one's network provides for a "surrounding field of friends and relatives who help give his life meaning, establish and maintain norms by which he regulates his behavior and protects him from the impersonal world."

Pattison (1976) attempts to define the social role of the mental health professional vis à vis intervention in different types of social systems. He outlines six types of social system intervention zones: the family unit, the intimate psychosocial system, the temporary psychosocial system, the ecological system, the kin replacement system, and the associational system. The first two include the nuclear family and their personal network of relatives. The third includes therapeutic communities, treatment centers, and hospitals. The ecological system includes community resources such as schools, churches, therapists, and neighbors. The kin replacement system includes self-help groups such as child or wife abuse groups, rape and divorce groups, and a variety of related support groups. Examples of the associational system include street corner gangs, professional and service organizations, church groups, and social clubs. Pattison suggests that the individual is connected to these systems in order of intimacy from most to least intimate, and that each system can serve its function by helping the individual cope at a given point.

One underlying theme in this book is that our lives, well-being, and ability to function on a daily basis depend on the quality and adequacy of our social support systems and on our ability to mobilize these systems, particularly during crises.

Caplan (1974) and Jones (1968) both indicate that our capacity to handle the stress in our lives depends on how effective our social support structures are. Caplan and Killilea (1975) make a strong case for the potential usefulness of the family and its extended network as a support system. Caplan enumerates a number of these family functions, such as serving as the source of ideology and guidance, as a problem solver, and as a validator of identity for all its members. In his social policy recommendations for future planning and service, Caplan basically suggests a networking process that will encourage and promote the "intactness, integration and mutuality" of the extended family.

Much of the literature in this area points out the strong relationships that exist between emotional health and supportive social networks. Bell (1962) found that sick and well families had different kinship relationships. Alissi (1969) and Feldman and Schertz (1967) reported that families seeking treatment report ineffective social networks. Hammer (1963) found that ineffective networks showed a high correlation with mental health admissions. Kleiner and Parker (1974) measured the degree of importance and alienation of an individual from the family network, the friends' network, and the co-worker network. Their measures of impairment were history of mental disorders, self-esteem, and pyschoneurotic symptom score. Their findings indicate that alienation from the family, friends, and co-worker networks was related to their measures of impairment; the degree of alienation and impairment varied with the importance of the network.

Pattison (1976), using his psychosocial scales, found that his sample of neurotic subjects indicated that the neurotics had an impoverished psychosocial network of 10 to 12 people, which did not provide a supportive psychosocial matrix. His psychotic population was found to have only 4 to 5 people in their network, quite a small and ineffective network support system. Pattison's data provide additional evidence that demonstrates that mental illness is related to the quality of one's supportive network.

In studying the social network resourcefulness of psychiatric patients, Tolsdorf (1976) found that his sample of hospitalized patients experienced fewer intimate relationships and more stress with their family networks prior to hospitalization. These patients had not utilized their family and social support systems to the extent that other nonpsychiatric ("medical") patients did. These medical patients were able to draw much more significantly on their social and family support systems during crises. Based on his data, Tolsdorf further delineates two orientation sets, positive and negative network orientations, and concludes that all of the psychiatric patients in his study demonstrate a negative network orientation compared to the medical sample, which had a positive network orientation.

Numerous clinicians have indicated the importance of the extended social network in clinical practice and in family therapy. These clinicians include Auerswald (1965), Hansell (1967), Boszormenyi-Nagy and Spark (1973), Pattison (1976), Garrison (1974), Erickson (1974, 1975), Attneave (1969, 1976), Speck (1964, 1967), Speck and Attneave (1963), Speck and Rueveni (1969, 1977), Rueveni and Speck (1969), Rueveni (1975, 1976), and Rueveni and Wiener (1976).

Of particular interest is Garrison's application of the social support system with psychiatric patients. Garrison (1974) describes a technique for "receiving, assessing, planning, linking, and monitoring people in crisis." This screening-linking-planning (S-L-P) method brings together the family and social networks of the individual in crisis prior to, during, and following hospitalization periods; the S-L-P method provides an effective and supportive network.

Garrison describes a number of successful interventions by the caregiver staff of the psychiatric hospital who mobilized the patients' social networks to cluster around the patients, reinforce positive expectations, develop options for managing the crises, and maintain contact with the patients during and following the release from the hospital. Garrison reports effective mobilization of the social network of chronic patients hospitalized for long periods of time. With slight modification of staff expectations, such patients can be weaned away from the hospital and can live adequately in the community. The assembling of the network might provoke a crisis with such patients; the crisis is needed to overcome resistance to change and to cause the patient to rely less on the hospital staff and more on the supportive social network of family and community.

Callan, Garrison, and Zerger's (1975) work in mobilizing the social support network for residents of drug dependent persons shows its usefulness, particularly prior to the residents' reentry to the "real world" and during an in-house crisis (spouse wants divorce, father's death).

In a recent study, Garrison (1976) reports the benefits gained in mobilizing the social support network for elderly persons during times of crisis.

Sarason and his colleagues (1977) have described their efforts to develop the triuniversity network; in doing so they have demonstrated an excellent rationale and insight for the utilization of the network concepts and process as well as its practical applications in noncrisis situations. Their minute descriptive narration of the development and implementation of their project is a valuable source of information pertaining to the often untapped human resources and opportunities for growth that are available when the networking process involves commitment and collaboration on the part of different people willing to reconnect their efforts.

Erickson (1975) views networks as useful for curative groupings of individuals, as a location of resources, an interpreter of help-seeking behavior, and as a mitigator of the effects of multiorganizational involvement with a family. Erickson further states that "if the concept of network offers anything for clinicians other than an expansion of family therapy, it must be shown that additional assessment and treatment ability can accrue to practitioners by developing and expanding the concept." In an earlier paper (1974), he describes a service network intervention combined with continuing family therapy as one example of expanding the concept of network.

Clinical experience gained from work with a variety of family crises indicates the desirability and efficacy of mobilizing the extended social network for supportive and healing functions.

Speck (1964), describing his early work with the families of schizophrenic patients, noticed the absent member maneuver, when one or more family members would absent themselves from therapy sessions. His home visits and his later insistence that the family assemble their extended system of relatives, friends, and neighbors were attempts to replenish the family system with additional energies and support that would help in breaking the therapeutic impasse. In collaboration with Attneave, an experienced family interventionist, six network phases were identified, and further applications of utilizing the social network for support and healing were described (Speck & Attneave, 1973).

Attneave (1976) describes the excitement that can be generated during a network intervention session and concludes that, "Indeed, working with people who are in relationship to one another, family and nonfamily together, seems more logical than groups of 'intimate strangers. . . . ' " From these perspectives she concludes that "it is logical to utilize a range of therapeutic interventions based on the full range of relationships operative in real life."

Haley (1976) maintains that networking, whether naturally or socially engineered, binds humans together in purposeful activity that satisfies our social group survival needs for collective action. She further states "that socially engineered constructs are replacing natural networks of extended families, tribes and neighborhood systems that were predictable, dependable and easily identified with. Group identity seems to be as important to humans as individual identity, and the more fragmented the social order, the greater the need for constructed networks."

Bleisner (1976) states that "the effect of family networking is to establish and encourage the development of common cause relationships . . . the clarification of existing networks within a community makes response to public crisis quick and effective."

In my own work with various families in crisis (Rueveni, 1975, 1976), the mobilization of the extended system of family and friends continues to be of paramount

importance. This mobilization of additional energies in-
fuses the dysfunctional family system with an intimate community of caring people who can become involved with
their concerns, maintain temporary support, and activate
or reactivate additional options for solving difficult family
crises.

These networking efforts are based on a frame of reference that emphasizes the importance of family and
friendship systems. When the extend.d family system is
intact but is dysfunctional (as is the case with many family
problems), the networking efforts are mainly directed toward helping such a system to become less dysfunctional by
increasing the communication among its members. The
increased communication can mean the opening up of old
and new family issues that have not previously been discussed or shared within the formal extended family structure. The outcome of networking such a family system
often results in a new, more productive pattern of relationships among family members. These new family commitments may be forthcoming particularly when the crisis in
the family is of increased intensity. Such efforts at networking the family system may not always be productive in an
immediate amelioration of the crisis, and further efforts are
usually made by the ailing member to seek relief and help.

When the extended family system is minimal or nonex-
istent, the networking efforts could be directed toward the
development of a substitute family system consisting of
nonfamily members such as friends, neighbors, and others
who could become involved with the family in crisis as a
temporary social support system.

The networking efforts described in this book include
both systems, the family and its larger social support components. These efforts, which are directed toward crisis
resolution with the nuclear family by mobilizing natural
and reconstructed social support systems, depend on an
effective formation of small support groups that continue

their supportive functions after the formal intervention sessions. When members join the support groups, they usually invest time and effort in helping family members with specific tasks and activities that may lead toward a change in the present crisis. Many network members mirror the general cultural values of heavy dependency on the professional and his or her ability to help solve problems. This dependency can contribute to the lack of interest or motivation on the part of network members to continue their efforts beyond the formal network sessions. The networking process helps to identify the more active and concerned members, those willing to give time and effort in joining a support group for one or more of the family members in crisis. The durability of these natural and reconstructed social support systems following the family networking process is an important aspect that contributes to the healing process of family members.

Research studies identifying the effects of family network intervention on the family system are needed. One such effort has been under way by Marc B. Goldstein,[1] who collected data in an attempt to answer the following questions.

1. Is there evidence of successful crisis resolution following family network intervention?
2. Are there changes in the frequency or quality of interaction between members of the network?
3. Are there any changes in the degree of the cohesion/alienation felt by the network members?
4. Are there any changes in interpersonal perception by members of the nuclear family and their network?

The outcome of this and other studies can provide additional avenues for understanding the nature and process of the social network as an effective support system.

[1]Personal communication.

Chapter 2

THE NETWORK INTERVENTION PROCESS

Family network intervention is an attempt to mobilize the social network support system in a collaborative effort to solve an emotional crisis. It is a time-limited, goal-oriented approach that will help family members in crisis to assemble and mobilize their own social network of relatives, friends, and neighbors; this network will become collectively involved in developing new options and solutions for dealing with a difficult crisis. This intervention process includes an intervention team that rapidly involves networking of the family members with its extended social support system in a process that can result in modifying destructive relationships and in the development of temporary support systems for one or more of the ailing family members.

THE HOME VISIT

The home visit allows the network interventionists and the family members to meet and discuss the feasibility of mobilizing the network support system. Whenever possible, this "screening" session should be conducted at the home. However, various circumstances may result in such meetings being conducted at other locations, such as a relative's home, a hospital, or a clinic. The home is the preferable location, since it is the prime natural habitat of most family systems. Meeting at home reinforces the team expectations that preference is given to the home as the place where their friends and relatives may be called to convene if necessary. The home meeting is, for many families, a convenient, less stigmatized place to convene than, for example, a psychiatric facility, where reinforcement of the "sick" role models may be expected by some families and some network members. The home visit permits the team to become familiar with the concerns of the ailing family. The information gained from this session usually is the basis on which a final decision can be made as to whether or not further networking efforts are to be made. The session also allows family members to become familiar with the team members' expectations and to experience the networking process and their own roles in such a process.

The home visit takes close to 2 hours and could best be described as a mininetwork session that usually includes most of the network phases. The home visit frequently is attended by members of the nuclear family and does not include additional network members. On some occasions, a few family relatives are invited to attend. The decision as to the attendance of additional family or friends during this initial home visit is mutually made by prior consultations between the family and the team leader, who feel that the presence of these individuals may add additional information regarding the nature of the crisis.

The process that develops during the home visit is similar to that of a fully attended network intervention session. The difference between the two is the existence of a larger number of people who become involved in the networking process, helping to mobilize each of the network phases fully, and the goals of the session. The goal of the home visit is to determine to what extent mobilizing the family network will provide the best intervention modality.

In a later chapter, a screening session is described where the family is interviewed in a hospital setting and a large number of staff attend. The screening session served both the goals of evaluation for networking and a first network session with both staff and family members in attendance; it enabled both staff and family members to obtain firsthand information about the networking process by becoming involved in such a session prior to mobilizing their own family network.

During the initial phase of the home visit, a retribalization process takes place; family members meet and get to know team members. After this, the team leader outlines the purpose for the meeting. He or she must share with the family previously known information gained from the referral source or other sources. Family members are told that additional information will be needed so that a decision can be made one way or another.

Each family member is encouraged to share feelings about the nature and scope of the problem. This activity usually leads quickly to a polarization phase, where family members disagree; they maintain their own points of view as to who is at fault, who promotes conflicts, who maintains resentment, who takes sides, who blames who, and who is being "scapegoated." The team may have to explore these issues in order to understand the nature of the dysfunctional relationships. Family members tend to continue in their usual patterns that promote the conflict, and the team members must be aware of their own goals and remain sensitive to the hurt and frustration that members of the family experience while sharing those feelings.

The session may become temporarily mobilized if the family members feel that there are hopes and solutions available without mobilizing their support systems. The team needs to explore further any previous efforts that were attempted by the family members, either individually or collectively, to solve the problems. If such efforts were used, they must learn of the success or failure of the members in solving their problems. As the team continues in its efforts to obtain information about the family, they may find the family members feeling resistant and hopeless. During this depression phase, the team has to acknowledge the experiences that the family members have and learn what the difficulties are. When the team members persist in focusing on the nature of the relationships among family members, the underlying reasons for the lull in activity and the feelings of hopelessness can come forward. Usually there is a family secret or similar painful material that is difficult for the family to deal with openly. The team needs to encourage the disclosure of such painful material. When such a disclosure can be dealt with during the home visit, it usually leads to an exchange of feelings that can bring family members out of the depression phase into a mini-breakthrough.

The breakthrough is not meant to imply that the crisis is over. Instead, often it may mean that both family and team members can better decide if assembling their support system is the next course of action. Decisions concerning the desirability of having a network mobilized can usually be agreed on by the team and the family during the home visit.

Sometimes the team as well as the family needs additional time to discuss other options, and arrangements can be made to delay a decision until after the home visit. When the team feels that the family crisis does not justify family network intervention, either because the degree of family desperation is not sufficient or because insufficient preparation and efforts have been made by the family in dealing with their concerns, the family members are encouraged to attempt to seek other help. Names of individuals or agencies that could offer help should be given, and a follow-up can be made by team members later on.

When the network seems to be an appropriate avenue of intervention to the team, but family members are hesitant to decide, the team should provide to the family all information concerning the steps involved in the process, reading materials, and telephone contacts for future consultation and decision. Many families need time to discuss the implications of calling on their network support system for help. Team members can help the family during this phase by providing all available information.

When the decision can be reached mutually by both team and family members to attempt networking the family and social support systems, the team helps each family member to develop a list of family and friends. A date for a meeting is determined, and final arrangements are made regarding financial reimbursement, videotape permission, and another location for the session if the home is not selected as the preferable location.

The family members are given help from the team as to what statements they may wish to make when inviting their network to come to their home. A typical call should include a brief statement of the problem and of the need for the network members to come and participate in a network session to help the family solve its problem. When the plans are being made to videotape the session, the invited network members should be told in advance about the possibility of being recorded and that written permission will be needed from the participants. The advance information should include a statement that the network member is considered to be important to the success of the session and that his or her participation may help in making the session a successful one. Invited members must also learn about the networking process, and they should be informed of further reading materials that will enable them to become familiar with networking. The family members may invite their network by phone, by letter followed by a phone call, or just by letter. The team members could be helped in developing their strategy and the follow-up efforts when a full list of the network participants, including names, relationship to the family, addresses, and phone numbers, is prepared.

CRITERIA USED FOR FAMILY NETWORK INTERVENTION

Mobilizing family network support systems seems to be appropriate for a wide variety of dysfunctional relationships, particularly with family disorganization resulting from attempted suicide, depression following family break-ups or separations, several so-called "psychotic" behavior patterns, and self-destructive symbiotic relationships.

The criteria for selecting the network approach includes the nature and scope of the crisis, the degree of family desperation, previous efforts made to deal with the problem, the availability of a sufficient number of resources such as family and friends to assemble, and the willingness of the family members to call on these resources for help.

Network intervention, as defined above, is mostly appropriate with family concerns that have been difficult to modify by other therapeutic interventions. Previous experience indicates that for family members treated either in individual or family therapy, the network can provide an excellent modality for gathering sufficient energy to overcome the difficulty. The inclusion of others in solving the problems gives each family member appropriate support in finding ways to deal with a previously desperate situation. The more desperate the members of the family are in seeking solutions to the problem, the better the chances for the network to succeed. We often refuse to conduct a network if there is not sufficient interest or motivation on the part of the family members to get involved in solving the problem as a family unit.

An additional consideration is whether there are enough extended family members and friends available to come and participate. The average family can usually assemble between 40 and 50 people without much difficulty. However, in many cases, very few family members are available. In such cases, if the nature of the crisis justifies the assembly of a network, consideration could be given to mobilizing only friends and friends of friends to serve as an alternative and temporary "second chance" family support system.

Finally, the question of family willingness to assemble the network is vital. Some families in crisis who could benefit from the network approach find the process difficult to accept. They would rather deal with the problem piecemeal. The public exposure and the sharing of painful feelings is too much for them. These feelings are understandable, and the decision to assemble the network is left up to the family members. However, in some cases, one can find both parents agreeing to the network, and their younger son, the "identified patient," refusing to attend. At times, one parent is supportive of assembling a network, while the other is fearful and rejects the idea. In such cases, it is best to go along with the majority of family members. The network is not assembled for the benefit of only one member; it is a collaborative effort for the entire family system. The team members can suggest a polling of votes and go along with the majority. A frequent consequence of this is the refusal of one or more family members to attend. This is fine with the intervention team. As long as some family members do express the need for a network, the professional team may wish to support their efforts. Those family members who threaten to boycott the meetings rarely carry out their threats. They will hide in the room, or leave the house prior to the network and then appear in the middle of the session, declaring that they have changed their minds. In a recent network, the "index patient" hid throughout the network session in her parents' garage, but later came in and hid in the basement. A small support group finally went to be with her, while the rest of the network proceeded with the remainder of the family members.

Further discussion of the location for the meeting, seeking possible permission for videotaping the sessions, and financial arrangements all can and should take place at this first home visit. Fees are usually determined by the amount of time the team spends. Experience indicates that each network session usually requires 6 to 8 hours of work, including preplanning, leading the main session, and following it up.

THE NETWORK PHASES

Experience in assembling family networks confirms Speck and Attneave's six distinct network phases. The phases are *retribalization, polarization, mobilization, depression, breakthrough,* and *exhaustion-elation.*

The initial *retribalization* phase occurs when the assembled network makes contact with each other; people usually mill around, meet other people, acquaint themselves with new people, and reconnect with old members of the family whom they may not have seen or heard from in a long time. The team's task at this initial phase is to facilitate rapid connections, familiarity, and readiness to participate and increase the level of involvement. Milling around the room, followed by activities that allow for the expenditure of some physical energy such as jumping up and down, clap-

ping of hands, screaming, and whooping can help the network begin to function rapidly in a more cohesive fashion.
The leader and the team involve the network in forming a
circle and singing some favorite melodies in unison.

After a brief outline by the team leader as to the goals
of the network and the need for involvement on the part of
each individual, a short period of time is allotted for identifying each of the network participants and their relationship to the immediate family. When this is completed, the
team usually suggests that the immediate family members
take a place in the center of the room; they are encouraged
to outline briefly the nature of the crisis as they view it and
their own expectations and needs from the assembled network of family and friends. For many in the network, this
is the first opportunity to learn about the problems
firsthand as they are seen by all family members. Since each
family member views the crisis in a different fashion, most
of the issues begin to polarize around the differing perceptions and feelings expressed by the family members. Some
network members begin to take sides with one or another
family member, bringing the network process to its next
phase, polarization.

Events that take place during *polarization* are important
to the unfolding of the network process. During this phase,
the network participants become involved firsthand with
members of the family; they contribute their views and
feelings with regard to the nature of the crisis. The team's
task during polarization is to *discourage* dependence on
them as professional problem solvers and to *encourage*
greater participation, sharing of concerns, and sharing of
differing viewpoints from everyone. The team may suggest
often that members sit in close proximity to the family
member they feel most supportive of or, while expressing
their views, identify of which side of the family they feel
most supportive. Some members may find this difficult.

However, encouraging sidetaking can help in getting continued involvement, and this allows the next phase, mobilization, to take place.

The exchange of various issues concerning the crisis allows for the formation of the network "activists," the individuals who begin to initiate collaborative efforts at solving the crisis. If there are enough network activists available, the network becomes mobilized. The team must facilitate the process by encouraging specificity of action so that a number of smaller groups can be formed to discuss further the problem at hand.

Mobilization is usually followed by a temporary lull in activities that causes members to feel somewhat discouraged by their inability to find immediate solutions to the problems. This phase, *depression,* can result from the difficulties and frustrations of many in the network who feel that their contributions are not being accepted and that their hopes for crisis solution may take longer than expected. This phase is marked by a temporary feeling of "going in circles," increased tension, boredom, and frustration. The team's task during this phase is to encourage the members to acknowledge that they feel frustrated and "stuck" and to suggest making additional efforts. It is frequently necessary for the team to find additional techniques to bring about a greater awareness of the family's problems. During this phase approaches such as sculpting, encounter, Gestalt, and other psychodramatic-type techniques may be chosen by the team to use with the immediate family members. Timing, however, is of utmost importance in obtaining maximum results for breaking the impasse during the depression phase.

Some networks remain stuck in a depression phase or even begin with a depression phase, which makes it more difficult for the network process to unfold. The skills of the team members at this period in helping to mobilize the network cannot be overemphasized.

After depression, a *breakthrough* can take place. This phase is usually characterized by increased activity and feelings of optimism and encouragement. The events that allow the breakthrough to occur are mainly due to the continued efforts of the network membership and its activists, who relentlessly continue to contribute and share by becoming involved with family members and with each other in their concern and support. This phase is primarily characterized by the feeling on the part of many members that there are workable solutions and that their contributions and efforts are paying off. Breakthrough often begins before the formation of the support groups, or it may follow this event. During this phase the team must help members to identify which support group they are willing to serve on. The network is usually formed into smaller support groups that meet in various locations in the home.

The final network phase is *exhaustion-elation,* a period where many in the network feel satisfaction and accomplishment.

THE TEMPORARY SUPPORT GROUPS

The critical factors that contribute to crisis resolution among family members are the activities and commitments that develop from the formation and continued efforts of the temporary support groups. These groups assemble to help each of the members of the family. As an example, in a family of four (two parents and two children), four support groups will usually form, one around each family member. The support groups continue the events that took place during the first network, translating them into specific goals and tasks so that each support group member can make helpful contributions. The support group members must report their progress to the entire network at the next meeting.

Support group members make arrangements for future meetings and keep telephone contacts with the family members, with each other, and, if necessary, with the team. Their function is to discuss, plan, and help carry out additional alternatives available for crisis resolution. Support group members are usually those network activists who are willing to mobilize their own resources in a collaborative effort aimed at finding alternative living arrangements if required, finding a job, and offering financial help, community resources, friendship, and social contacts. Members of the support group plan additional meetings that will take place after the completion of the network. They continue individually to maintain telephone or face-to-face contacts as frequently as possible while maintaining communication with the rest of the family and continuously seeking to consider options, and they offer help during the critical period that follows the network meetings. The vitality, motivation, interest, and sense of collaborative commitment in those support groups can only come from the network activists. They must give their time and invest their efforts in helping a family member to solve a difficult problem. Experience indicates that it is difficult to maintain a high level of commitment in the support groups for long periods of time. Most support groups report a decreasing level of involvement as the crisis abates, a time span that varies from 3 weeks to 3 months or more.

MOBILIZING THE NETWORK SUPPORT SYSTEM

The following cases provide examples of families experiencing various difficulties in their relationships that lead toward a crisis that was dealt with by mobilizing their network support system.

CASE 1. THE BLUM FAMILY NETWORK

Network intervention can often help to bring a dramatic change in a desperate and depressed family system by altering its previously self-destructive relationships and by providing constructive alternatives for dealing with the crisis. The sense of urgency and crisis resulting from an attempted suicide by a family member can be overwhelming, and yet assembling the network of family and friends in an attempt to solve such a crisis can mobilize the system for involvement, support, and caring, resulting in crisis resolution. The Blum family is a case in point.

Susan Blum, at 26, felt depressed and lonely. Since her recent divorce, she had attempted suicide on several different occasions. Efforts at family therapy including Susan, her parents, and her younger sister and brother did not lead toward significant crisis resolution. The family's increased sense of desperation and helplessness, intensified physical and verbal confrontations during therapy sessions, and the ongoing sense of crisis were some of the factors that made network intervention an appropriate referral.

After a home visit, two network meetings were planned; the time of the first meeting was scheduled to coincide with Susan's threat to take her life. Over 50 family and friends came to the first meeting.

Following a high-energy retribalization phase, with the people getting acquainted and reacquainted with each other, the meeting went into a high level of involvement by many in the network. Strong support was shown toward each parent by his or her own family of origin.

The phases of polarization and mobilization took place, followed by a longer depression phase. Mrs. Blum's feelings of disappointment with her husband's inability to be more firm and take responsibility, her feelings of rejection by her daughters, particularly Susan, and Susan's own feelings of increased anger toward her mother all con- tributed to the lack of progress and the network's inability to break the impasse.

The network moved toward a breakthrough phase when members of the family were able to specify what they needed and expectated from each other and from the net- work members. The intense confrontation, particularly be- tween Mrs. Blum and Susan, provided the network members with the first opportunity to offer help and to begin to consider alternative options in handling the crisis. Three support groups were formed, one around each of the parents, and one around Susan; her sister and brother took part in Susan's support group. The support groups met during the week and reported increased contacts; many members felt that their contributions were construc- tive and helpful to members of the family.

During the second session, Susan shared her increased need for friendships and for further support in finding a new place to stay, in finding a job, and in making additional social contacts. She reported that her suicidal feelings ebbed away, primarily because of the numerous calls from friends and family and the constant feeling of support she had experienced following the network session.

During the second network meeting, additional efforts were made by the professional intervention team to help both parents to face and deal directly with their lack of communication, their needs from each other, and their willingness to reconnect with the many family members and friends in their efforts toward a better relationship and family harmony.

A periodic follow-up of the Blum's network a year later revealed that immediately after the second network, Susan was able, with the help of her support group, to find a new residence, find a new job, and become more and more involved with many friendships and social contacts. Al- though the Blums did not continue as a family in therapy,

Susan was reported to be making significant progress in individual therapy.

CASE 2. THE GROSS FAMILY NETWORK

The results of network intervention can be significant in affecting changes with cases of self-destructive, symbiotic relationships. The case of the Gross family provides an example of utilizing the network process, the intervention team's inventiveness, and the network activists' resourcefulness in achieving a separation between a mother and her 26-year-old son, resulting in benefits to the entire family system.

Jerry Gross was hospitalized a number of times for so-called "psychotic breaks." At 26, he lived with his mother, who claimed that their relationship was burdensome to her, particularly since the death of her husband a number of years earlier. Family therapy with Jerry, his mother, and his sister Linda usually resulted in continued and constant blaming by Mrs. Gross of her son; she complained about his refusal to work and his lack of consideration for her in her own efforts to help the family survive.

The ongoing conflicts between mother and son interfered with Linda's professional and social life. She quit nursing school, felt depressed, was unable to leave home, and felt guilty if she did. Both of the family therapists reported an increased sense of frustration in their efforts to change what seemed to be a strong, symbiotic bond between mother and son. The therapists' own sense of helplessness and frustration in their efforts to help the family was noticeable. The referral for network intervention was made in the hope that the revival of the Gross family network could help both mother and son to separate from each other, and also enable Linda to resume her social and school efforts, which had deteriorated as a result of the family conflicts.

Two network sessions were scheduled. The family was able to call on 30 relatives and friends. The remainder of the network consisted of family therapy students and invited professionals who were interested in the network process. During the first session, most of Jerry's family, particularly his mother and aunts and uncles, scapegoated him to the point that he decided to leave the session. The network was polarized around the issue of the family blaming Jerry instead of offering alternatives for dealing with the relationships between the three family members. When Jerry returned to the session, a sculpting experience designed to help the three family members identify the most difficult areas of their relationship was developed by members of the intervention team.

While mother and son stood shoulder to shoulder, sister Linda was asked to "sandwich" herself between them; she was encouraged to push out, but was unable to do so. Linda acknowledged the reality of the experience of feeling "stuck between mother and brother" in their fights. The intervention team suggested the formation of a tight circle of people who attempted to prevent first Linda and then Jerry from breaking out of the circle, an experience designed to help both of them symbolically break out of the home. First Linda and then Jerry were able to push themselves out of the circle, expending considerable energy while doing so. The investment of energy by many of the network members during this experience mobilized the network and provided an opportunity for the intervention team, with the help of the network activists, to attempt to "cut the cord" between mother and son.

The "funeral ceremony" followed. Jerry was asked to lie flat on his back, was covered with a white sheet, and was pronounced dead. Mrs. Gross, kneeling beside her son, was encouraged to mourn him, as were the other network members. Clasping both hands, crying and moaning, Mrs. Gross began pouring out her feelings. She wanted her son to leave home, find a job, and let her live her own life peacefully. She then revealed an important piece of information that she had never before been able to express. "My father on his dying bed said to me, 'Wait, this boy will be a success, not a failure' " and "I promised him that I would carry it out." Her inability to let go of her son was partially connected to this vibrant promise that she made to her own father to be a good mother and daughter, to stick with it, and to help Jerry at whatever cost. Many of the network members were able to express their feelings of support for Jerry and his mother during this period of mourning. The first network meeting ended with many more people becoming involved in offering Jerry, his mother, and his sister alternative options to consider.

After the second network meeting, Jerry was able to accept the suggestions from members of his support group to find a place to stay and to explore the possibilities for a job. However, the weeks immediately following the network were difficult for both Jerry and his support group to deal with. Jerry went through a series of "testing" behavior patterns proclaiming that nobody loved him anymore, that his mother and the network caused him misery by suggesting he go and live elsewhere. At one point he called the local suicide prevention center, identified his previous psychiatrist by name, claimed that he was about to kill himself (but did not reveal his own name), and hung the phone up on the operator. It took some time until Jerry was identified as the caller and the support group members were alerted; they visited Jerry's new apartment, only to find him safe and unharmed.

A few days after the completion of the second network, Jerry attempted to return home, only to find that the locks on the doors at his mother's house had been changed by his mother with the help and inventiveness of her support group. Unable to enter, he finally returned to his own apartment. As the weeks passed, Jerry expressed the need to continue in therapy, and he was seen on an outpatient basis. His support group was composed primarily of some of the professional people who felt sympathetic toward him and a few family members.

While Jerry's support group was not fully mobilized, his mother and sister were reported to be making significant gains since the network meetings. Mrs. Gross sold her house and moved to a smaller apartment, and she was making social contacts. She was able to accept the fact that her life would be much more joyful without constantly checking on her son's whereabouts. Linda was reported to be continuing her schooling and having a social life. A recent followup with Jerry found him gainfully employed, calling on his mother once weekly, living in a halfway house, and continuing in therapy on an outpatient basis.

CASE 3. THE JONES FAMILY NETWORK

The following case represents a collaborative effort on the part of the family division team members of a local mental health center, the Jones family, a black family of seven members in crisis, and myself.

Mr. and Mrs. Jones live in North Philadelphia in an area generally populated by black families and some Puerto Rican families. Both parents recently became concerned about the bizarre behavior of their 29-year-old daughter, Cynthia. Cynthia previously worked as a secretary but, after returning home from a vacation in Europe, became depressed, reportedly over a disappointing love affair. She barricaded herself in her parents' front vestibule wearing a thick coat; she refused to leave, wash, or move out.

The mental health team, headed by a psychiatrist, vis-

ited the family in an attempt to formulate possible treatment for Cynthia. The parents were ready to court commit
their daughter. However, the mental health team members
felt that the Jones family network could be a worthwhile
alternative. When the network idea was suggested during
the home meeting, attended by both parents and Cynthia,
her 21-year-old brother, and her three sisters, who are all
married and live away from home, Cynthia declared that
she was interested in telling the entire family of her concerns. The network meeting was scheduled to be held at
the Jones' home.

The room was quite small but crowded with many
family members, friends, neighbors, and some of the Jones'
church congregants, including the local minister. The main
goal for the network was to help both parents in their own
efforts to find alternative options to hospitalization for
Cynthia. The network team consisted of myself, the referring psychiatrist, and three black mental health professionals.

During the session, issues such as the lack of communication among family members was expressed by Cynthia's
three sisters. Cynthia, in particular, felt angry at her father
for not caring and angry at her mother for not comforting
her. The parents, on the other hand, were concerned about
Cynthia's inappropriate behavior, which embarrassed them
in front of the neighbors, and about her lack of motivation
in finding a job.

The team efforts were directed toward mobilizing
other family members and friends to offer Cynthia another
place to stay. One of Cynthia's aunts emphasized that while
Cynthia stayed with her, at her own house, she behaved
appropriately. Support was given for Cynthia to move out
of the vestibule.

At the end of the session, Cynthia's aunt offered to
have Cynthia come and live with her for a while, and
Cynthia accepted this offer. The mental health team made

arrangements to continue monitoring the family and Cynthia and to make themselves available in case of future crises. Reports from the Jones family indicate that following the network, the family members began making additional efforts at meeting together more often to increase their level of communication and awareness of each other's needs.

CASE 4. THE DURAN FAMILY NETWORK

A critical factor in mobilizing the network for action is the investment, efforts, and commitments of family members to share their concerns openly with the entire network and become involved in the network process and the support groups that follow it. When collusions exist between parents, or when the family and its network system are not desperate to change the status quo, the network cannot be mobilized, and little change can occur. The Duran family is a case in point.

Twenty-one-year-old Jim was hospitalized following his ongoing depression and attempted suicide which, according to him, resulted partially from the divorce of his parents. While father remarried, mother did not. Jim felt that his parents' concern over him might bring them together again, particularly since his father remained on intimate terms with his mother even after their divorce. It was difficult for Jim to express his anger toward either of his parents, and most of the time his affect was low.

Therapy with Jim was a slow process, producing little change in his abilities and confidence to leave the hospital setting. The network approach was suggested to Jim, who was willing to try it, provided his parents could participate. Both parents were initially reluctant to become involved with the network process, but finally agreed to try it. The network should not have been encouraged at this point, since neither of the parents felt sufficiently desperate to justify assembling the network. Their own entangled relationships and the distrust on their part to share with others were warning signals to proceed cautiously with the network approach. However, the intervention team probably felt the need for the network, regardless, and two sessions were scheduled.

The first session ended with a depression phase where the immediate family members, including Jim, his parents, and his three sisters were not able to share their concerns effectively to mobilize the activists for action. Although support groups met between sessions, they reported little progress during the second session. Some movement was made when Jim was able to face up to his father and express his feelings of affection for him. Both parents were ineffective in unfolding their real concerns with each other, and with Jim blocking major efforts on the part of the support groups to become involved with them, little change followed the meeting.

Both parents saw little use for their support groups. Jim's support group was mobilized initially to meet with him in the hospital but, after a brief period, they became aware of his refusal to change his pattern, particularly when he realized that little change was made by other members of his family. The inability of the immediate family members to become involved with the network resulted in no change for the Duran family and in mobilizing the network to help Jim leave the hospital.

Chapter 3

NETWORK INTERVENTION WITH DIFFICULT FAMILY CRISIS

THE COHEN FAMILY NETWORK

The two network sessions undertaken by the intervention team were designed to help the Cohen family mobilize support from their extended system of family, friends, and neighbors to help them in their efforts to stop their daughter's self-destructive acts. The aim of this network was to help both parents and daughter develop an appreciation for each other's needs and concerns, working toward new options involving the family crisis.

There were four members in the Cohen family, both parents in their early fifties, their son, Allan, age 28, married and living away from home, and their 22-year-old daughter, Diane, living at home and having a great deal of difficulty in her relationships with both her parents. In the past few years Diane, who was depressed, had frequently attempted suicide, primarily by drug overdose; as a result she was a frequent patient in a variety of hospitals. Attempts at individual and, later on, at family therapy did not provide sufficient changes in the malfunctioning relationship between Diane and her parents. Both parents were quite desperate to save their daughter's life, as well as each other. Mr. and Mrs. Cohen have experienced heart problems and their emotional crisis was causing additional stress on both of them.

The referral for family network intervention came from the family's therapists, who felt that by mobilizing the Cohen's extended family system, additional energies could be brought forward by the network to help in resolving the crisis. During the screening interview, the team members became convinced that the Cohens were unable to solve their crisis by themselves and, that by mobilizing the Cohens' network, there was a good possibility that Diane might consider other more constructive alternatives than killing herself. Two network sessions were planned. Two dates were set, and the Cohens proceeded with calling on their family and network of friends to assemble for the first session.

The leader assembled three team members who met to plan their initial strategy. A number of factors were to be considered prior to the first network meeting. One team member, a physician, expressed his concern over the additional stress that could develop from the network process and its effect on the parents' previous heart problems. The family physician was contacted and briefed as to the family's decision to attempt network intervention. The family physician felt that the network idea could help instead of hinder the Cohens' heart conditions. He argued that they both were angry and unable to express and share many of their feelings; the network, he felt, would help them to relieve the pressure and consequently be medically desirable.

Other considerations in planning the team strategy were the need to mobilize the Cohens' network in a rapid fashion so that support could be given to Diane in exploring alternative options in relating to her parents other than by provoking and attempting suicide.

The First Network Meeting

During the first session, many members found it difficult to become involved with the immediate concerns of the Cohens, since the family members were initially unable to become specific and spell out their needs for the network. The leader and his team attempted on a number of occasions to intervene by encouraging openness and involvement, but met with little success.

As the session progressed, polarization occurred. Mrs. Cohen, with the help of her three sisters, continuously defended herself and her husband and pointed her finger at her daughter, whom she felt was the main problem for the family. Because of the polarization, members were unable to come together and work toward a breakthrough of the crisis.

The team urged the formation of three support groups to continue their efforts between sessions with Mr. Cohen, Mrs. Cohen, and Diane. The team met during the week between sessions to plan additional strategies to mobilize the Cohens' network toward a possible breakthrough.

Several goals were considered. First, communications between Diane and her parents had to be further opened up. Diane was angry at her parents, and an opportunity had to be provided for her to express this anger in a productive instead of a self-destructive manner.

Another observation made by the team during the first network session was that death was an underlying concern of all of the Cohen family members: the parents' feelings about Diane's frequent suicide attempts and potential death; their own feelings about their own deaths resulting from their heart problems; and Mrs. Cohen's strong feelings about her own father, now deceased who, according to her, "If he were only alive would solve all the family's problems." The spirit of the dead father was felt during the first session. The four sisters frequently mentioned him as the possible "rescuer" and powerful healer. He was, as one sister stated, "Our Rock of Gilbraltar."

A final point in considering an effective intervention strategy was another observation by the team that Mrs. Cohen frequently compared her husband and Diane to her own father, usually ending up with neither one being able to measure up.

The team strategy planned for the second session was to help Diane in confronting her parents and to follow up the experience with the "death ceremony." It was felt that these two experiences could help the network become mobilized for a possible breakthrough.

The Second Network Meeting

Most of the people attending the first meeting returned for the second meeting. The meeting began with reports by the three support groups; each outlined some constructive discussions, but all indicated a need on the part of Diane and her parents to deal with their conflicts.

A confrontation developed between Diane and her father, with Diane angrily accusing him of telling his friends that she did not pay her share of money for the network. "How much do you owe me?" asked Mr. Cohen. "I am aware of how much I owe you," retorted Diane. "You are not honest with me. You make me feel that I am still a little girl," she continued. "What is the issue?" asked one team member. "The issue," responded Diane "is my father telling his friends that I am not responsible while he refuses to talk to me as a mature person." "How about being responsible for your own life?" screamed Mr. Cohen at his daughter angrily. Diane kicked the chair and, looking at her father, said, "I do not have to please you." One of Diane's aunts stood up, her face pale, and said, "Diane, it looks to me as if you have to make your father angry to get the love you want from him. Why make him angry if he is willing to give it to you?" "Because," screamed Diane, her eyes filled with tears, "for 22 years he was not able to give me any love. The only way I received any love from him was by provoking him." "How about killing yourself?" a team member asked Diane. "Only when I get close to death do he and Mother care," said Diane. "You are full of baloney," Mr. Cohen responded.

Another team member suggested that both Diane and her father could look at each other's eyes, stop screaming, and move toward each other, expressing their feelings nonverbally. For a moment both stood apart; then, reaching for each other, they embraced, sobbing and comforting each other.

The team members felt that although both were expressing some tenderness, the anger between the two and the lack of direct involvement by Mrs. Cohen were still important issues to be dealt with by the network. The leader of the team felt that there was a need for greater involvement by other network members with the family. To allow for a rapid involvement, the team planned the strategy of "killing off" first Mr. Cohen and then Diane. The rationale for doing this was based on the following observations. First, death was an important health issue in the family, because both parents had previous heart problems and because of their frequent concern about Diane killing herself. Another important issue for this family was Mrs. Cohen's feelings about her dead father who, if he had lived, would help her and the family to cope with the crisis. Mrs. Cohen's sister felt that perhaps Diane's problems began when her own daughter died at age 11 because Diane was such a close friend of hers at that time.

We agreed to mobilize the network by utilizing the funeral ceremony. Diane's "death" evoked many feelings of sympathy toward her from many network members. Both of her parents expressed hope for change in their relationship.

The network became mobilized when Mr. Cohen was "killed off." As Mr. Cohen was covered with a sheet, Diane was asked to kneel beside her "dead" father and express her feelings toward him. Diane began sobbing. "I only wanted you to love me," she softly whispered. Mr. Cohen, unable to keep still, pulled the sheet from covering him and reached out to hug his daughter again. "Why do you let her do this to you?" screamed Mrs. Cohen at her husband. "She knows you love her." Sitting beside her husband now, she began confronting Diane. "Not having a father is like being dead," Diane angrily told her mother. "What do you mean not having a father?" asked Mrs. Cohen. "Having a wife that took his balls away. That is what I mean," Diane replied. "You do it to him and to me. You always compared me to your own father. I never measured up to his standards or yours," Diane continued, angrily accusing her mother. "You are looking for excuses, Diane. You are not going to put a wedge between your father and me. How about taking responsibility for your own problems?" Mrs. Cohen continued, confronting her daughter.

Both parents were on the offensive now. "What do you want from your daughter?" the team asked Mr. Cohen. He replied, "We gave her much more that she could ever give back to us. I want her to be healthy, not to get in trouble, and to stop killing herself." Diane responded by saying, "I want you to love me, Dad. The only time I get attention from you is when I try to kill myself." "I always loved you," said Mr. Cohen. Tearfully, Diane said, "You don't understand. I wanted you to listen to me, to be with me, but you were always busy."

A team member interjected, "She really intimidates you, Mr. Cohen." "Yes, she does," replied the father. "How?" he was asked. "By talking above my head," he replied. "She is intelligent, but she never could come down to my level and talk to me. I feel stupid compared to her. If she could only come to my level, but she always talks about her books and ideas. I could never get involved with her on this level."

As father continued it became clear how inadequate he felt on an intellectual level when comparing himself to his daughter and how angry he was at her for frustrating him by attempting to kill herself and upsetting him and his family.

Mrs. Cohen similarly felt angry at Diane, but determined to keep the distance between herself and her daughter. Weary of her daughter's manipulative pattern, she was expressing the need for additional help on the part of others in the network to help her and her family.

As the impasse lingered on, many in the network became restless. "I want help to get through to my parents," said Diane. "We want you to help us handle Diane," both parents responded. The three support groups decided to convene once again. Many ideas were discussed and developed.

As the second network meeting came to an end, the three support groups were actively engaged in networking their members, making plans for future meetings, and considering alternatives for helping the family.

Our follow-up of the Cohen family found both parents making significant improvements in their own relationship. Although there was a period following the network where Diane was not making any significant progress, with the help of her support group and additional therapy, she decided to try living in an Israeli kibbutz for 6 months; upon returning to the United States she found a job and was reported to have stopped her suicidal patterns completely.

Thus, the efforts to mobilize the Cohens' network paid off. These efforts began during the first session, were continued by the support group members between sessions, and were intensified during the second session. The intense confrontation between Diane and her parents provided the network activists with an opportunity to learn, firsthand, of the nature of the relationship between Diane and her family. The parents, on the other hand, felt relieved at this opportunity to share their difficulties. The response of many of the family and friends was warm, accepting, and supportive. One indication of the parents' ability to manage their lives better following the network was a decision on their part to take a vacation together, leaving no telephone or address where they could be reached. In the past, Diane would often time her suicidal attempts to coincide with her parents' plans for going away. Diane herself was able to continue in therapy, following the network, in a more productive fashion and later, became gainfully employed and socially active.

THE QUINCY FAMILY NETWORK[1]

The Quincy network was mobilized to provide family members support in managing their 14-year-old daughter, Betty. The main goal of the intervention was to help separate mother and daughter, at least temporarily, providing an opportunity for both to rely on their social support system.

Mrs. Quincy contacted the network intervention team because of family problems that mainly involved her inabil-

---

[1]Portions of this case, titled "Treating the family in time of crisis," were published in a modified form by Ross V. Speck and myself in Jules Masserman's *Current Psychiatric Therapies*, 1977, 17, 135–142

ity to manage the behavior of her 14-year-old daughter, Betty. She had taken Betty to several psychiatrists, but Betty was uncooperative, blamed the psychiatrists for her difficulties, and refused the numerous medications that had been offered. Finally, the whole family had been put on megavitamin therapy by the last psychiatrist seen, and he had made a diagnosis of schizophrenia and hypoglycemia and advised a diet for Betty.

Mrs. Quincy, a fortyish woman who looked much younger and seemed more like one of the children, was the mother of Jane, 17; Bill, 15; Betty, 14; Jerry, 12; and Dorothy, 9. Mr. and Mrs. Quincy had recently been divorced, and Mr. Quincy lived in a different city with the woman he was about to marry.

A striking feature of the family unit was the hopelessness and exhaustion in all family members. Betty had dropped out of school some months previously. She refused to bathe, did not eat with the family, stayed up all night and then insisted on quiet during the day so she could sleep, left rotting food hidden around the house, and constantly littered and dumped garbage about the house. At times she attacked her mother or Dorothy.

In the family therapy sessions Betty would sit mumbing or complaining about the family; her hair completely concealed her face, except when she rubbed her eyes with a mixture of water and spittle, which she kept in a jar in her purse. Jane and Bill gave much of the history and behaved in a parentified way. Both said that they could not take the tension and disruption in the home. Both wanted to move out. Jerry wanted to move in with his father. Dorothy was frightened of Betty, but wanted to stay with her mother.

About six family therapy sessions were held. Mr. Quincy attended one of these meetings. He tended to blame Mrs. Quincy for not understanding Betty, for having been absent in the past, and for being a slovenly housekeeper. He was glib, used much denial, and could not be convinced that Betty showed any symptoms of a psychotic disorder. He also seemed like one of the children.

Because of the amount of family disorganization and total exhaustion, network intervention was suggested to help build up support systems for each family member. An additional factor was the 3-hour drive that the family had to undergo to come for therapy.

A single 4-hour family network intervention was planned in their home. Mrs. Quincy and the rest of the family were asked to compile a list of all the people they knew who might be willing to meet in their home to help change their predicament. Mr. Quincy was also seen with his new wife. They agreed to attend, and Mr. Quincy's sister was invited from a distant state. Mrs. Quincy invited her parents and several of her siblings from out of state. Mrs. Quincy, Jane, and Bill invited their friends. By the time of the meeting, 10 days later, they had invited over 60 persons.

The intervention team consisted of six persons; Dr. Speck and I acted as team leaders, our spouses as group process consultants, and a young psychologist as trainee and process consultant. An audiovisual expert videotaped the network intervention.

The team arrived at the family home at 7:00 P.M., about 1/2 hour before the meeting was to start. A few of the invited network members had already begun to arrive. We made a tour of the house and selected the living room and archways spilling into the hall and into the dining room as the space to be used for the main session. We met with Betty, who refused to attend and who was hiding in the garage. She said she might listen to the meeting from the basement, where there was an "escape" door. A team member was assigned to get written permission from everyone for videotaping. Only one couple refused "because they were in politics." After a consultation with Mrs. Quincy, they were encouraged to leave, since it was doubtful that they would be of help anyway.

By 7:45 P.M., 60 persons had arrived, and we decided to begin. After a brief retribalization, we made a simple statement to the assembled network outlining the purposes of the meeting. We pointed out that the Quincy family was exhausted, that their friends, neighbors, and relatives should begin to think of ways to help the various family members, that support groups for each member would have to be set up, and that the group could help in making the Quincys' divorce more effective. (Mr. Quincy had been appearing unannounced for dinner, criticizing Mrs. Quincy's housekeeping, and taking pictures of the interior of the house, which he threatened to take to the public health department.)

Each network member was asked to introduce himself or herself and tell his or her relationship to the network. Then the Quincy family was asked to sit in the center of the group and tell the group what the trouble in the family was and what they hoped from the network intervention.

Betty remained in the garage and later in the basement. The team decided not to force a frightened and hostile 14-year-old to sit through a long session. She would undoubtedly have tried to escape, and the resulting disruption would fragment the network instead of uniting it as a functioning social system.

Jerry said that he could not stand being called "dirt" at school and that he wished he could have a chance to live with his father "to see if he liked it there." Jane said that it was impossible to live in the same house with Betty, and that she wanted to move out to California or go to college. Bill said he was sick of Betty drinking out of milk and juice bottles and of her smelling up the house. He, too, would like to move. Dorothy said the house would be all right if Betty were not there. Mrs. Quincy said she could no longer put up with Betty and wanted help in getting her into a school. Mr. Quincy said the problem with Betty was exaggerated and that Mrs. Quincy, with her untidy housekeeping, was the real problem.

The polarization phase had now begun. I began to confront Mr. Quincy about inconsistent statements he had made. The polarization continued about whether Betty was sick and about blaming Mrs. Quincy for the family problems, and it then focused on the unresolved divorce between Mr. and Mrs. Quincy. At this point the larger network was called on for their reactions to what had happened in the meeting to this point. The majority of the network was very supportive of Mrs. Quincy, and there was some hostility toward Mr. Quincy. His new wife became very angry, took his side, and attempted to align Jerry with herself and Mr. Quincy. She invited Jerry to come live with them.

A few network members began to make suggestions about school or new living arrangements for Betty. This began the mobilization phase of the meeting. At this point, the intervention team asked the assembled network members to each pick one of the seven Quincy family members and to form a small group to discuss in greater detail what assistance might be needed. The small groups met for the next hour in different rooms in the house; the intervention team members "sat in" or "floated" from group to group. Each group chose a member to report back later to the entire assembled network, in summary form, the results of the small group meetings.

After several hours of group work, there commonly is a feeling of depression-resistance that appears when the work of polarization and mobilization is met with a sense of frustration and difficulty in solving the tasks.

When the groups reported back, there were numerous suggestions about different alternatives to help individual family members. The groups volunteered to act as committees who could be turned to over the next several weeks for advice and help. An aunt offered to take Betty into her home with her own children. A lawyer present suggested that Mrs. Quincy needed legal help to get Mr. Quincy not to barge into the house whenever he felt the need. A teacher offered to help Betty prepare for her Grade 8 exams. An artist offered her art lessons. Many offers were made to other individual family members. It was pointed out that the unresolved divorce between Mr. and Mrs. Quincy threatened Mr. Quincy's new marriage, and marital counseling was recommended.

As the meeting ended, Betty appeared (after having met with her small group) and offered to go with several people to get pizzas. The team left at this point, but the network stayed together discussing what had happened until nearly 2:00 A.M.

The breakthrough and exhaustion-elation-termination phases were combined in this single-session network intervention. The main manifestation of these phases was the group's "high" feeling of having accomplished something and of having set up support groups to work with any family problems.

Our follow-up of the Quincy family a year later revealed that significant changes had occurred in their daily lives. Betty, who was offered a place to live with her aunt in another state, accepted the offer. After about 10 weeks she began causing too much trouble and was uncooperative, and arrangements were made for her to attend a residential school. Later she returned to live with her aunt and attend school there. She was reported to be making friends and social contacts. Mrs. Quincy and Betty talk to each other over the phone each month.

Mrs. Quincy changed jobs and continued for a while in therapy, where she reported to be feeling a difference in her life since the network was completed. The rest of the family seemed much relieved. Jane started college and the other children returned to school. They were all able to make new friends and, although their sister, Betty, was away from home now, they felt closer to her than ever before. Mr. Quincy seemed much happier, and his new marriage seemed intact.

THE NASH FAMILY NETWORK[2]

There are occasions where a family cannot mobilize its extended system to assemble in time of crisis. Experience with families who have little or no extended system of relatives to mobilize suggests that networks of friends and friends of friends can be equally effective in providing the needed support for change. The Nash family network was primarily assembled by most of Mrs. Nash's friends and a group of family therapy professionals coming to a workshop on network intervention, thus becoming involved with the Nash family as a supportive and effective network, that mobilized themselves to help the family in their time of crisis.

There are three members in the Nash family. Mrs. Nash is a divorcée in her late fifties and a recovered alcoholic. She lives in a small apartment with her two daughters, Joan, 32, diagnosed previously as "paranoid schizophrenic," and Linda, 24, who has had cerebral palsy since birth. Another daughter died at 3 months from suffocation. Mr. and Mrs. Nash were divorced 15 years ago. Mr. Nash, now dead, was an alcoholic and had served time in prison for embezzling funds. When the two girls were growing up, there was open hostility between their parents,

[2]Portions of this case were published in a modified form under the title, "Network Intervention: The Key Role of Network Activists," by myself and Muriel Wiener in *Psychotherapy: Theory Research and Practice*, 1976, **13** (2).

and an incestuous relationship took place between Mr. Nash and Joan. It has been a constant struggle for Mrs. Nash to keep her family together, considering the extensive loss and trauma suffered by each family member.

Since Mr. Nash died about 10 years ago, Joan was able to work for a brief period as a medical technician, but she made a serious suicide attempt after a broken engagement and was hospitalized for 3 months. When she left the hospital, Joan became increasingly withdrawn and rarely left the family apartment. She refused to work or socialize with friends. Dissension in the Nash family was intensified by Joan's behavior.

The three women complained about their inability to separate from each other. Joan stated that, "We are glued together." They reported being fearful of the outside world and dependent on each other. Yet the anger and resentment toward each other increased daily to a point where each member felt that her life was becoming unbearable. Some solution for the crisis had to be found.

The Nash family had been in family therapy for 4 years before Mrs. Nash and Linda were seen by Mrs. Wiener. Mrs. Wiener saw the two women for 6 months. Joan refused to come. No significant change had occurred during that time, and Mrs. Nash was becoming more and more desperate. Joan, she said, was "driving her to an early grave." She felt helpless and was tearful and depressed most of the time. Linda found her position as "peacemaker" between her mother and sister intolerable.

The Need for a Breakthrough

It was quite clear that the Nash family's dilemma was difficult, and no solutions were to be found easily. The intensity of the daily confrontations between Mrs. Nash and Joan and the desperation that each of the three women experienced were sufficient to consider another approach. The focus of responsibility for change in their malfunctioning family system had to be shifted from the therapist to an active and concerned group of family members, friends, and neighbors who could become actively interested in helping change the Nash's destructive mode of relationships by intervening and supporting each of the members to find her own individuality, and primarily to help each to achieve the long needed separation from the others.

Basically we were opting for a network intervention approach whereby this concerned "tribe" or network of "activists" would take the responsibility for finding as many alternatives as possible for the Nash's to consider, adopt, and follow through.

Assembling the Tribe

During several family therapy sessions, the network idea was explored with the family. Joan began to come to the sessions to discuss some of the requirements that had to be met. It was the Nash's responsibility to call and invite their own family and friends and to make arrangements for space, since their apartment was very small, and for video-taping.[3] This was a major difficulty for the family because they had virtually no extended family. Joan had no contacts with other people, and Mrs. Nash had a minimal social life. Linda had many acquaintances and friends through her active participation in a cerebral palsy association. The family made a gigantic effort to assemble a network and succeeded with encouragement from the therapists. Two network meetings were planned. The first was conducted as part of a workshop demonstration in family network

[3]The first of the two scheduled meetings was to occur at a large hotel conference room; it was scheduled as a network demonstration and was attended by workshop participants and involved family members.

process. The second meeting was held in a large room of a sheltered workshop residential facility provided by Linda's friends.

The First Network Meeting

About 70 people attended the first network meeting. It was held in a large room. Many of the participants were not familiar with the Nash family, since they were only attending the workshop. For the first meeting the Nash family were able to assemble about 20 friends and neighbors, one of whom was a close family member. A small number of professional consultants were invited to serve as additional resources.

The intervention strategy during the first meeting was aimed at sharing the Nash's problems with the entire assembled network. Our aim was to initiate a process whereby the members could work as a more cohesive system as a result of their shared experiences (retribalization), and to encourage different and often conflicting network members' feelings to surface (polarization). Our efforts were to continue to mobilize the network activists (mobilization) for support and involvement (overcoming group depression and helplessness) for a realistic and constructive breakthrough.

Our role as network intervenors was to serve as a resource for the members, to guide the network process, and to intervene at strategic phases of the network process. This role demands a great deal of sensitivity to the process of group interactions, a willingness to confront, and a considerable amount of experience in dealing with people in a crisis situation.

After a brief retribalization ceremony (whooping, hand clapping, swaying) and an outline of the family's problems by the intervenors, the Nash family members were asked to role play a typical dinner table conversation.

Mrs. Nash was confronted by Joan. Each of them repeated their familiar statements reflecting their anger and disgust with one another. Linda expressed much helplessness and self-pity. The seating arrangements were then shifted. The family sat in an inner circle surrounded by their network. Mrs. Nash was sharply criticized by her sister-in-law. She blamed her for not being a capable wife and mother, and for neglecting most of the family's advice on how to raise the children when they were young. This stirred up a considerable amount of group discussion and support for each of the three women by many of the network members.

The most critical event during this first meeting was the emergence of a small nucleous of network activists, some of whom did not know the Nash family previously, but who were quite willing to listen openly and be ready to continue in formulating alternative solutions. The network members were encouraged to participate in the meeting and to consider ways of actively helping the family.

During the first meeting, we observed the network going through the network phases outlined earlier with the exception of the breakthrough.

The Second Meeting

The Nash family assembled over 50 people for the second meeting. A significant number were Linda's friends, and some were Mrs. Nash's old friends and neighbors. Others were those individuals who had attended the first meeting, became quite intensely involved in the painful drama as it unfolded, and decided to participate and try to help one or more of this family.

The meeting began with a brief period of network news, attempting to bring all members up to date on most significant events of the week (rumors, secrets, telephone calls) concerning the Nash family. Network members were then asked to make a choice as to which one of the three women they felt motivated toward, interested in, or able to help the most, and to join in a group with that family member. Three support groups formed: Mrs. Nash's, Linda's, and Joan's. Each support group consisted of about 16 members. They were instructed to be able to report later to the entire network on concrete, specific, alternative solutions that they had considered and agreed on for their family member.

The three support groups met for about an hour. The activity in each group was different, but the participation was enthusiastic and intense in each one.

In Joan's group, exploration for a job and a residence were initiated. A number of members had job possibilities for her. A nonverbal activity was instituted. Joan was instructed to shut her eyes and consider herself dead; each support group member then expressed some feelings about her. At the completion of this powerful experience, Joan was visibly moved. A number of members invited Joan to dance while the entire group clapped hands and joined in. More discussions followed.

Joan's support group had accomplished a great deal. A large number of activists came up with job offers, there was an invitation to spend two weeks with a network family, and various other social invitations were extended.

Mrs. Nash's group was very supportive of her position. There were offers to become reacquainted with old friends, promises to see each other more often, and a pledge for active, continued help and support as long as she needed it and was willing to receive it.

Linda told her support group that she wanted a job for Joan and a meaningful job for herself. She wanted to move out of the apartment. Offers of jobs and a new residence were also actively explored with Linda.

The meeting ended in a hopeful atmosphere. Names and addresses of all attending members were recorded, and the group was encouraged to keep in contact with the

Nash family either by phone, mail, or subsequent monthly meetings.

The Follow-up

Three months after the network we mailed brief questionnaires to all network members. We also kept contact with the family by telephone and through the network grapevine.

We learned that Joan did not return home after the second network meeting. She stayed with the family of an activist network member. She was offered and accepted a position as a housekeeper for an elderly and wealthy woman. Joan reported significant improvement in her relationships with others and an active interest in socializing again as a result of her support group's work.

Linda was still living at home and working part-time; she reported an increased interest in dating and more confidence in herself. Plans were being made for her to enter a girls' residence in the near future.

Mrs. Nash reported significant changes in her present attitude toward life: "I feel relaxed for the first time in years. I can't believe this has happened."

The three women reported telephone calls, visits, and letters from some of the people in their respective network support groups. They also felt that these active members were and will continue to be a valuable human support system that provides each of them with much confidence, hope, and reassurance whenever they needed it. The network activists were able to accomplish what years of therapy had been unable to do for the Nash family.

We were quite interested in the comments and feelings of the network members, particularly the active ones. We asked them to fill out a questionnaire. The following four questions were asked: (1) How did you feel about the network experience? (2) In what way did you contribute to this effort? (3) Have you kept in contact with the members of the family (specify phone calls, letters, meetings)? (4) What suggestions do you have for continued work and support for the Nash family?

All responses to the first question indicated the dynamic and intensely moving experience that they had participated in. Responses to the second question indicated personal commitment to help the Nash family. To the question of keeping in contact with the Nash family following the network, most respondents expressed a continued interest in the family through face-to-face meetings and by telephone calls. Suggestions for continued support included establishing a monthly network newsletter, having a monthly network reunion, and continuing contacts among all the network participants.

NETWORK INTERVENTION FOR A THERAPIST AND HER PATIENT

A symbiotic relationship can often develop between a therapist and a patient, making it extremely difficult for the therapist to discontinue the therapy when it is appropriate to do so.

The network in this case was assembled by both patient and therapist. The therapist, a psychiatrist in her forties, had been practicing for over 15 years with a good reputation for effectively handling difficult cases. Her patient, Tom, was a clinical psychologist in his mid-thirties who had difficulty maintaining a job for any length of time. He lived with his former college teacher, a widowed man in his sixties. Tom was a loner, drank a lot, and was easily irritated. He visited the therapist three times a week, and reportedly was looking forward to the therapy sessions. The therapist liked Tom and over the years felt that the affectionate bond between them had helped to some degree in the therapeutic progress of her patient. However, as therapy continued and Tom continuously found it difficult to maintain a job and make additional progress, the therapist felt that therapy should be discontinued. She felt she had given all she could, and perhaps a change to a different therapist would be more beneficial for Tom. The therapist felt that Tom had difficulty in separating from her as well as from his friend, the college professor.

The therapist discussed termination with Tom, who refused and pleaded for a continuation. When the therapist insisted on discontinuing the therapy, Tom became angry and proceeded to destroy the office, attack the therapist physically, and slash his own wrist. The therapist was able to call the police, who finally subdued Tom. The therapist then felt drained and helpless. In a meeting at the therapist's office a week later with Tom and his friend, we began exploring the feasibility of assembling a network to help both Tom and his therapist separate. Tom did not have much family. His mother had divorced his father earlier, remarried, and now lived in a distant state. Tom claimed that he had not spoken to her for over 3 years. His attempts to call his mother to come to the network were unsuccessful. The team members contacted his mother later on and asked her to attend a network meeting, but she refused.

To mobilize support for Tom, a network of friends and friends of friends had to be assembled. A date was set for a network session. The objective of the meeting was to separate Tom and his therapist by providing enough support for both to do so. The team's strategy was to help the network membership develop a familiarity with the issues and provide various alternatives for helping both Tom and his therapist disengage. In addition to Tom's friends and friends of friends, some of Tom's former therapists also attended.

Some of the more critical issues brought out during the network meeting were Tom's earlier difficulties with his own parents, whom he felt rejected by. Tom's excellence in school, his frequent outbursts, and his inability to find a job and keep it were some of the issues that were discussed. The therapist was able to share with Tom and the network her own frustrations with Tom, her inability to see changes occur, and her decision to discontinue therapy. At one point the team arranged for Tom's former therapists to share their own frustration with Tom while he was in therapy with them. They all were able to agree that the pattern was similar and that they had experienced similar difficulties while working with Tom.

As a team we felt that the therapist should be able to share her feelings concerning her decision to discontinue therapy with Tom, and leave the network. When the therapist was able to do so, the network efforts were then directed toward finding other options available for Tom. At the conclusion of the network meeting, there were many who felt that Tom should explore moving away, finding a job, and attempting to maintain it for a while, and then seek a new therapist.

The follow-up on the case revealed that the separation between Tom and his therapist did take place, although Tom attempted to make some additional unsuccessful efforts to return to her. The support that the therapist received helped her to continue and maintain the separation. Tom felt quite angry at the team, blaming them for helping the therapist and not him. He reportedly was able to make some changes in his life following the network, and he now had available to him a larger support system if he wanted to take the opportunity to mobilize them in the future.

ON DISENGAGEMENT AND SEPARATION OF FAMILY MEMBERS

The process of network intervention with families in crisis often results in temporary or long-term separation from one's family. Increased family interconnectedness and the utilization of resources available within the social network for healing and support may sometimes require a period of separation between two or more people in the family who are in an intense conflict. When disengagement occurs and when the extended social system can be mobilized for support, dysfunctional relationships can be explored, and alternative options for change in the system can take place in time. It is not uncommon that periods of self-exploration and additional professional help can follow the network process, leading family members to utilize the energies and resources available within their support system to gain additional strength.

It is toward this goal of allowing family members to gain additional strength from the social support system for a needed disengagement that the network intervention team uses their experience and skills.

Chapter 4

THE THERAPIST AS A NETWORK INTERVENTIONIST

The therapist[1] who works with the extended system of the family will quickly discover that to function effectively within such a system, active and direct involvement will be required from him. To mobilize such a system of 40 people or more, the therapists need to time their intervention efforts to coincide with the particular phases with which the network is involved.

THE GOALS OF INTERVENTION

Each network has its general and specific goals to achieve. The specific goals depend on the nature of the problems

---

[1]The term therapist is used in this chapter to describe the functions of the network team leader.

with which members of the family have been struggling. The therapist learns about these concerns during the pre-network, initial home screening meeting with the family members and attempts to develop specific goals that usually can be modified as the events unfold during the sessions.

The general goals for network intervention are quite similar in nature. These usually are to:

1.   Facilitate rapid connections, familiarity, and readiness to participate, which increases the level of involvement and energy.

2.   Develop and encourage sharing of the problems and concerns by members of the immediate family, which allows for increased involvement and exchange of a variety of viewpoints by network members.

3.   Facilitate communication between the family and its extended network system, which emphasizes the need for network activists.

4.   Provide direct intervention and a deeper exploration of the nature of difficulty during impasse periods, which leads to crisis resolution.

5.   Assist in the development and formation of temporary support groups, which serve as resource consultants.

These general goals correspond to the six network phases outlined earlier. The therapist and his or her team are involved in system intervention and can become effective network interventionists; they mobilize the network for action and crisis resolution by involving the network in achieving these goals. The work of translating these goals into an effective network intervention process and strategy can be additionally understood by discussing the roles of the network therapist and his or her team.

THE ROLES OF THE NETWORK THERAPIST

The network therapist needs experience and skill in family dynamics, group process, and psychodramatic techniques. After frequent team consultations, the therapist times the specific intervention strategies to coincide with the events taking place during the process of networking. The therapist must be sensitive to the process at the nuclear family level of interaction and at the extended system level of interaction. Cues and clues for timing interventions are based on the nature of discussions that take place at these two system levels, the phase the network is working in, from feedback of other team members circulating around the room, and from personal clinical experience of what "fits" best. For example, when most members seem to agree on one point of view, or when the exchange of ideas and feelings concerning the problem at hand does not involve members taking opposing points of view, the network probably needs to polarize around conflicting, often opposing, viewpoints and issues. The therapist and the team need to promote this exchange, which can result in greater involvement on the part of other network members. Another example would be when the members seem bored, tired, and unable to break a specific impasse in their efforts to help the family. The therapist will identify the depression phase and, with the team, plan a specific intervention technique that could help break the impasse, providing the members with additional areas for exploration and possible crisis resolution. During any network session, the therapist and his or her team also function as network conveners, network mobilizers, network choreographers, and network resource consultants.

The Therapist as a Network Convener

The therapist and members of the team function as network conveners primarily during the home visit or the retribalization phase. Although the responsibility for assembling a network is primarily that of the family members, the therapist functions as a helpful resource in outlining ways of developing family maps, or lists for assembling the extended system of relatives, friends, and neighbors. When the task of convening the extended system becomes difficult for some families because of little remaining family, the therapist helps in considering the convening of friends' networks and friends of friends' networks. In the case described in Chapter 3 the request for convening a network came from Mrs. Nash, who was interested in exploring the possibilities of assembling a network to help her deal with her 32-year-old daughter (labeled "paranoid schizophrenic"), who was living at home with her and causing her a great deal of anguish. She could not assemble more than a dozen family and relatives, since many in her family, including her husband, had died. The therapist offered this family an opportunity to participate in an upcoming workshop on networks that was to convene in their town the following week. The 50 network participants became a "family" support group for a day. Most of them returned to participate in a second network session the following week, thereby making additional efforts to provide support and help for resolving her crisis.

The Jones family network (Chapter 2) is another example of how the therapist provides help in the role of network convener. A network meeting was about to take place in the Jones' home in an attempt to help both parents to deal with their 29-year-old daughter, who had barricaded herself in the front vestibule, refusing to leave, eat, or sleep. Only 20 people showed up for the meeting. The team leader went outside and recruited a number of neighbors who were willing to convene and participate in helping the family at their time of crisis. The therapist and team were also able to call on the local minister and members of his congregation to come and participate in the network session immediately after the service that Sunday after-noon. The outcome of the network resulted in a develop-ment of a support system for the young woman, who was then able to move out and live with her aunt.

Another more direct role of the therapist as a network convener can be observed during the beginning of the main network session. During the retribalization phase, the therapist must provide network members with the opportu-nity to interact, share, and get acquainted with each other. People mill around the room; some have not seen each other for quite some time and others wonder why they were invited; there may be cliques; the initial activity may be that of a small group interaction. During this period, the need is for an increased collaborative development of the net-work energy level that will enhance further network retrib-alization and help members to activate additional energies for involvement. The therapist must develop a sequence of activities, some verbal and others nonverbal, that will per-mit the development of the retribalization phase to take place rapidly. This is done by providing network members with an opportunity to engage in energizing activities such as milling around, stamping their feet, screaming, and sing-ing in unison, followed by more relaxing activities such as standing in a circle, holding hands, closing their eyes, and humming silently.

The therapist's role is of a network convener working to increase a network's "energy level" and state of readi-ness for further involvement in the network process. It is entirely possible that during this phase and perhaps during the entire network process the network therapist is per-ceived as taking the role of a celebrant, a term coined by Zuk (1975) that connotes a role traditionally given by fam-ily members to clergy for initiating a healing ceremony.

Additional experiences with various forms of retribali-zation indicate the potential usefulness of this phase for bringing powerful emotions to the surface in cathartic fashion. A similar experience is reported by Katz (1976) in his interesting description of the healing ceremonies of the !Kung Zhun/Twasi healing dance ceremony, a collaborative effort that involves the whole community to release healing energy.

Another example, from the Blum family network (Chapter 2), further details this convening role of the network therapist. The therapist and his team began the retribalization phase by suggesting to members of the immediate family that they lead the entire network in a favorite medley of their choice. They chose the song "Sunrise, Sunset" from *Fiddler on the Roof.* As the rest of the network joined in, Mrs. Blum began sobbing and was held by her husband as the rest of the network was getting ready to deal with the unfolding family problems.

The therapist can often encourage other network members to help by acting as network conveners. In a network assembled on Friday evening at the home of a Jewish family seeking to stop their son's suicidal attempts, the retribalization phase began with the son's cousin, a rabbinical student, who was asked by the team leader to initiate the meeting by lighting the candles and offering the blessing; this was followed by the traditional welcoming of the Sabbath melody sung by the entire network. The cousin, utilizing the traditional Jewish religious ritual, was able to retribalize the network quickly.

The Therapist as a Network Mobilizer

Little can be achieved during any network session unless the network can become mobilized for action. The therapist and his or her team can and should be able to stimulate and encourage maximum participation and disclosures, sharing of conflicting points of view, and open dialog. In doing so, the therapist cannot be passive or uninvolved. To mobilize the network rapidly, the therapist frequently takes sides, confronts family or network members, and encourages clear communications and disclosures of painful feelings or secrets.

During the mobilization phase, where the potential exists for the formation of the network activists (those who strongly feel the need to provide support), the therapist needs to provide further support for additional exploration of the crisis. When the network members seem "stuck" or feel that their contributions are not being taken constructively by members of of the immediate family, a temporary phase of depression develops. During this phase the therapist needs to structure additional experiences that will lead toward a deeper exploration of the crisis (see The Therapist as a Network Choreographer).

The following vignettes further elaborate on this role of the therapist. During a recent network session, members of the immediate family had some difficulty in sharing their concerns openly. They spoke in generalities and were unable to outline specific issues. The therapist queried the family as to whether or not there were any secrets in the family. One of the uncles indicated that he wished he could share some, but his wife prohibited him from doing so. The therapist and his team insisted on discussing this issue, whereby the uncle was able to disclose the absence of one family member who was not invited; he also brought out the issue of his own feeling of being excluded from important family events. The therapist helped both the uncle and the network to mobilize their resources to deal with that specific issue.

During another network session, some of the relatives felt uncomfortable with the process. One uncle threatened to punch the therapist in the nose. When invited to do so, he left the room and then came back and shared his initial frustration and anxiety. An aunt seemed unable to speak directly to the patient and had to be reminded by the therapist on numerous occasions to speak directly to him, in the first person, with no lecturing. At another point during the same session, an argument developed between two cousins as to the nature of previous help provided by each of them and their past interests in the family's problems. The therapist encouraged self-exploration. At one point he took sides with one and at another point showed appreciation for the efforts of the other. When a group of activists began to form around the young man who was labeled "psychotic," the therapist and his team repeatedly had to encourage and remind the group to deal with feelings and avoid scapegoating; he had to provide specific alternatives for discussion.

The Qunicy case (Chapter 3) provides another example. The Quincy network assembled to help the divorced mother, her five children, and their father to deal with the difficulty they all had in relating to the 14-year-old daughter who lately refused to attend school, take a bath, or cooperate with the family. She remained in the garage most of the time, causing a great deal of stress on all other family members. When the team visited the home prior to the network session, the girl was tied with a rope to the garage door, refusing to participate in the session. She was told that the network was going to be held with or without her, and that she was welcome to attend if she so chose. During midsession she was standing in the basement listening in to the events taking place upstairs. At the same time, one team member found a typed note on her bedroom door requesting from the network members various specific actions she would like to see take place in her life. The team arranged for a support group to go down to the basement and work further on the issues with her. The network was mobilized around these events, particularly when it became evident that the requests dealt with tutoring, moving away from home, and making social contacts.

The Therapist as a Network Choreographer

Papp (1976) describes family choreography as a method of actively intervening in the nuclear and extended family by realigning family relationships through physical and movement positioning. She further states that choreography allows the therapist to draw the system with space, time, sight, hearing, energy, and movement. This role is quite similar to what the network therapist is involved with during the intervention process. To facilitate transition from one network phase to another, the therapist must be aware of two interacting systems: the nuclear family system and the extended family system. When members of either system seems to have difficulty during the network process, the therapist and the team members need to develop active and dramatic techniques that can mobilize the network for further involvement by providing additional opportunity for a deeper exploration of the crisis. These active intervention techniques often involve direct encounter, family sculpturing, and psychodrama, which can give family members a setting for restructuring and realigning of dysfunctional and self-destructive patterns. These patterns can be examined within the supportive network atmosphere, where trust levels can be achieved and public sharing of such interpersonal concerns can be dealt with openly.

The following vignettes clarify this role of the therapist as a network choreographer. The Blum network (Chapter 2) was assembled to help the family members develop alternative options in dealing with their oldest daughter's frequent suicidal attempts after her divorce. Many in the family and the network felt depressed and unable to make progress in their efforts to help. The suicidal daughter and her sister seemed angry, but afraid to confront their mother. The therapist and his team felt that a confrontation between mother and daughter could mobilize the network for further involvement and action. A sequence of activities was developed to help bring the confrontation about. First, the daughter was asked to step on a chair and look around the room for people she would trust. She mentioned a few people, excluding her mother. Mother, sitting below and looking up at her daughter, began sobbing and sharing her feelings of loss of a relationship and her need to love her daughter. The daughter, while standing on the chair, was helped by the therapist and the team to confront her mother directly and seek specific issues that she could fight over with her mother. Standing on the chair, physically "higher" than her mother, the young woman looked at her mother and then expressed feelings of resentment toward her. When they faced each other later on, an intense exchange of feelings took place. The daughter, supported by the therapist, pointed her finger at her mother and yelled that she needed to be herself and she did not care to do what her mother wanted her to do. The mother screamed back at her daughter and then reached toward her in an attempt to hug her, crying that she did not want to lose her. At that point the team separated them and asked the family members to realign themselves either beside the mother or the daughter. Mother was joined by some of her friends, while the daughter was joined by her father and sister. The 16-year-old son refused to join either and hid in the kitchen. This confrontation helped both family and network members to explore further the nature of the relationship and the crisis that was related to it.

Another example of how the therapist functions as a network choreographer comes from the Gross network (Chapters 2 and 8). When the therapist and the team staged a "funeral ceremony" where the son was asked to lie on the floor and was declared "dead," his mother and later on the rest of the network members were asked to share their own feelings about him.

This "death ceremony" was choreographed by the

therapist to bring out the feelings of grief mother had to face in separating from her son. It also provided an opportunity for the network system to offer direct help to both the mother and the son in their efforts to disengage from each other.

Recent experiences with simulating family "death ceremonies" are encouraging in that they seem to elicit a great deal of energy, frequently revealing intergenerational conflicts and "hidden agendas" not previously brought to the surface. Katz (1976), reporting his experiences with the !Kung tribe, quotes their view that to heal one must die and be reborn. My experience with "death scenes" during family network sessions suggests that it can be a powerful tool that should be used selectively and timed for a specific purpose.

A final example comes from a simulated network assembled to help a depressed wife who was having difficulty in relating to her husband, whom she claimed was too "close to his own mother." The wife perceived that relationship as interfering with her own marriage. The therapist choreographed an experience that helped to mobilize the network for involvement and action. The first experience was created around the wife, who revealed that she never felt loved by her own mother. Her two sisters were asked to kneel beside her while she attempted to create a dialog with her dead mother, whom she pictured sitting in the chair in front of her. The experience was further enhanced by the local minister, who came to comfort the wife, and her two sisters; a group of network activists joined them to consider additional support and ways of dealing with her problems. The second experience concerned the husband's relationship to his mother. Some of the network members felt that both should be able to examine their relationship openly. The therapist was approached by the father for help in dealing with the issue. The therapist tied a rope around the man's waist and asked his mother to hold on to the other end of the rope. Many in the network, including the team, confirmed that that situation depicted precisely how both were relating to each other. When the man finally was able to remove the rope, he began sharing feelings toward his mother that he could not or would not allow himself to share in the past. The support groups assembled around the father, and his own mother made some constructive suggestions for their future relationship.

The Therapist as a Network Resource Consultant

Network members are able to begin and to formulate alternative courses of action in dealing with family crisis by dividing into support groups. The therapist and the network team encourage the formation of such support groups. Team members usually are expected to provide the initial leadership in forming such groups, but they are not required to become active members of such groups unless they, themselves, choose to do so. When these support groups form, usually toward the end of the first network session, they meet for various periods of time in between sessions and after the completion of the network meetings. The team is available to members of such support groups as a resource consultant on a variety of issues with which members of such groups struggle. The following are some examples of this role of the therapist.

Toward the end of a network session assembled to help both parents with their suicidal daughter (the Blum network, Chapter 2), the therapist suggested that the network members form into three support groups, one for the daughter, and one each for each of the parents, where each member could support the family member of his choice. Many in the network felt uneasy in taking sides. "We like all three of them," and "We would like to help them all" were not uncommon comments. The therapist and the team members insisted on the formation of the three groups. When the support groups formed, arrangements were made by the members to meet during the week. A support group coordinator was selected who kept in contact with the therapist and the team during the week to consult on a variety of issues relating to the support group's commitment to work with the family members that they were supporting. During the week another team member met with the daughter, in a resource-consultant role, and reviewed the network progress and her own future involvement in the second network meeting. The result of this meeting with the daughter was that, with the help of the team members, she was able to elaborate what she needed from her parents and from the network membership. This included her feeling that many in the network provided her with new social contacts that helped to lessen her suicidal feelings and increase her need for additional friends, a new job, and continued support. After the second network meeting, members of all three family support groups met for a number of months; they kept in contact with team members in order to provide suggestions and feedback.

After the completion of the Gross network, assembled to help the mother and her son cut their mutual self-destructive symbiotic relationship, the support group that assembled for the son had only a few family members. Most members were professionals and friends who felt they could be of help. The support group consulted frequently with members of the team about housing, further therapy, and social contacts. The commitment of the members was quickly put to a test by the young man who was encouraged to find a place to stay away from home. He took an apartment in the local YMCA, returning home later only to find that the locks on the doors of his mother's house had been changed by his mother on the advice of her support group members. The son paced outside of the house pleading to get in, but finally returned to the YMCA. He further attempted to put pressure on his support group members to convince them that he needed to be taken care of in a hospital setting. The following evening he called the local suicide prevention center, claiming that he had overdosed and that he was a patient of a certain psychiatrist. The psychiatrist was alerted and, being aware of the support group's involvement, called on them for action. One of the support group members, a psychiatric resident, visited the young man and found him not to be a medical emergency. For a number of months the support group members continued their efforts, providing social and financial help. For more than a year after the network there was improvement with no hospitalization or suicidal attempts on his part. The mother's and sister's support groups continued to make additional efforts at helping both mother and daughter.

The Therapist as a Network Strategist

The therapist's roles elaborated in this chapter require that the therapist be an effective strategist. The task of the therapist in family network intervention and, to a great extent, in family therapy, is to be an effective clinical strategist. In family therapy the clinical strategy depends on the background and frame of reference within which the therapist operates. Most clinicians utilize strategies to help their clients change. The therapist who serves as the leader of the network intervention team employs clinical skills to develop intervention strategies that will lead to the resolution of the family crisis.

The concept of the therapist as a strategist implies that the therapist is aware of his or her own need to shift ground, to mobilize parts of himself or herself that may need to be activated and reactivated. The therapist cannot remain inactive during the intervention efforts. His or her energies are directed, in collaboration with the team, toward a rapid mobilization of the family system; to achieve this goal, the therapist may need to utilize himself or herself and his or her skills, energies, talents, acting ability, and resourcefulness to be an effective interventionist.

Chapter 5

ISSUES IN FAMILY NETWORKS

REFERRAL ISSUES

Therapists engaged in helping families change need to become aware of the potential usefulness of the network intervention process in helping family members achieve this goal. Referral for network intervention is related to a number of factors that are associated with the therapist as well as with the family members themselves.

To refer a family for network intervention, the therapist must become aware of the specific problems and family concerns that could be effectively dealt with by mobilizing the network support system. He or she has to increase his or her own sense of familiarity and confidence in this intervention modality.

Referral for network intervention does not imply that the family failed in therapy or that the therapist was ineffective. It does imply that the therapist feels that, in order for the crisis to abate, additional resources have to be mobilized so that dysfunctional relationships can change as a result of the direct intervention by the family networking process and the resulting formations of the family support systems. The therapist needs to be aware that network intervention can be considered when the relationships among family members reach a crisis point, at which time the use of additional resources and efforts is justified.

The therapist's familiarity and confidence with this approach can be greatly increased by participation in a network session. Some of the therapists that took advantage of this invitation to participate (most invitations come from the family members themselves) report that they have been able to learn a great deal about the patient's family system and about the process of network intervention. When the referring therapist is unable to attend the network session, the network team needs to keep in contact with the therapist to provide information about the events that took place during the network intervention sessions.

Unless the crisis reaches unmanageable proportions, most families will insist on delaying their decision for mobilizing their network. The therapist can assist family members reach a decision by developing the network idea sequentially. He or she can suggest that for the next session both parents may wish to invite several of their family, perhaps their own parents, brothers, or sisters. When the family is able to achieve this goal, they could be encouraged to bring some friends to another session. The therapist may choose to visit their home, at which time a small number of relatives and friends could be invited to participate in discussing the family concerns and the feasibility and need for additional assembling of the entire system for support and help.

When the therapist wants to become engaged in the network intervention process instead of referring the family, he or she should discuss this possibility with the family and make every effort to assemble a team to assist in this task. Some therapists report they would rather refer the family than become engaged themselves in the intervention process, since their familiarity and related transference issues with the family prevent them from becoming effective network interventionists. Although this factor should be taken into consideration by the therapist, experience with a number of cases indicates that each case must be considered independently. Often the referring therapist gains the family's trust and could be encouraged to become a co-leader of the network intervention team. A number of family networks have benefited a great deal by this arrangement, because the referring therapist provided a great deal of input to members of the intervention team and, at the same time, helped family members to overcome their initial resistance to become engaged in the networking process.

A number of cases illustrate some referrals for network intervention and the decision made by both the referring therapist and the family members. In the first case, consideration for mobilizing the network was suggested by the therapist to a couple that he had been seeing for a number of years. The husband was struggling with a progressive multiple sclerosis condition that affected his relationship with his wife and his 17-year-old daughter. His refusal to accept help from family and friends made things difficult for his wife. The turmoil at home became intolerable when the nurse, who for several years had been taking care of him, decided to leave. The man would burst into temper tantrums, refusing to consider another nurse and insisting that she had to stay and care for him. The therapist felt that network intervention was appropriate, since it could mobilize the family and social support system to help the nurse disengage while others could explore possible alternatives to help both husband and wife cope with their concerns. During the screening sessions, the idea of network intervention was explored and a decision was reached by the family to assemble their network. The referring therapist was interested in serving as a coleader of the intervention team. The therapist's decision to take part in the anticipated network was particularly welcomed by the family, since they felt that he had gained their trust and would be available after the network session to continue work with them.

In a different case the referring therapist was familiar with the concerns of both the parents and their 21-year-old, depressed son. The son's depression and lack of a job and friends would trigger continual fights between him and his parents that affected the other children in the family. The therapist felt that network intervention could help mobilize a social support and friendship group around the son and around each parent. During the home screening session, the father expressed interest in mobilizing the network; his wife and son refused to become involved with mobilizing their large network support system. The referral for network intervention, followed by the home screening session, let members of this family become familiar with the idea of network as a possible future resource. It stimulated both parents to call on two of their cousins to share their concerns and to consider a future family reunion.

CONFIDENTIALITY

Pattison (1976) presents an excellent rationale for understanding the issues of confidentiality by contrasting briefly the "personal" and "systems" models of psychotherapy. He states that in "the 'systems' model privacy is antitherapeutic, for it is the public pressure, public response, and public support that enables the person to move rapidly back into his accustomed social functions."

In the "personal" model, "privacy is therapeutic since it allows the patient to explore alternatives without public pressure, without public response, and without public support."

When members of a family in crisis do decide to convene their network, they go public. When they cannot bring themselves to share their initial need for help with their own network of family and friends, the networking process cannot proceed. Convening the network requires family members to begin a public process where confidentiality regarding the immediate concerns is difficult, if not impossible, to maintain.

The process of discussing family concerns publicly requires that the family members develop some degree of trust in each other, their social network, and members of the intervention team. The therapist and the team cannot guarantee that confidentiality could be maintained exclusively among the attending network members. During the home visit as well as during the network sessions, the therapist reminds the family that in order to deal effectively with the crisis, secrets should be disclosed and dealt with openly with the entire network. The issue of secrets is a sensitive one.

Families have secrets that usually relate to the crisis. Some secrets may be known to all family members, but they are not shared with anyone else in the extended system. Other secrets may be known to only a few in the family. It is entirely possible that secrets may not be secrets at all. Many family secrets are known to others in their network of relatives, friends, and neighbors, but are rarely acknowledged.

During the network intervention session, the therapist will usually encourage the family members to disclose secrets. The energy associated with secrets could benefit the network system, since it provides an additional stimulus for mobilizing the network for action. Members may acknowledge that they have known the secret for some time, but were unwilling to confront the family members for fear of embarrassing them or hurting their feelings. Many families who were able to share a secret with their network usually were quite surprised that instead of feeling embarrassed and ridiculed, as they had expected, they received warm support for risking expressing their feelings in the open. The support ranges from the offering of ideas for dealing with the crises in light of the new disclosures, to sharing of similar experiences by others in the network, who indicate how they have been able to handle their own dysfunctional relationships by sharing secrets.

The point of view advocated in this book is that the responsibility for directly disclosing secrets should not be that of the therapist or the team. Family members have the option and the right not to disclose secrets that they feel might be harmful to them. The therapist cannot and should not disclose these secrets, assuming that he or she may know them. This does not mean that the therapist and the team members are in collusion with the family. When secrets are not forthcoming, the team can suggest to the family during the session that it is their responsibility to bring additional undisclosed information into the open if they so choose, and that by delaying or being secretive the success of the network to become mobilized could diminish.

ON THE USE OF VIDEOTAPES

We have made an effort to videotape most network intervention sessions, primarily for training and educational purposes. The use of video equipment should be discussed with the family during the home visit. The family should be made aware that the tapes are to be used for professional, educational, and training purposes. When the family objects to the use of videotapes, each team has to evaluate its position about whether to undertake leading the session without recording it. It should be emphasized that video is helpful only when one has a training program where these tapes can be useful for demonstration of the network process and techniques of intervention.

When the family agrees to the use of video, they are requested to inform their network that video will be used and that written permission will be obtained. Before the network intervention meeting, each family and network member 18 years and older is requested to sign a consent and release form that indicates home address and allows the use of the videotape for educational and training purposes.

An issue that may arise after the network session is whether or not the network team should honor a request for erasing portions of the videotape where the parties involved are seen and heard. In the absence of a prior consent and release form, there is little that the team leader can do but agree to the erasure. When a prior consent and release form has been obtained, the team leader needs to explore further the reasons for the request. Inviting the person to view the tape may result in a cancellation of the erasure request. When insistance for erasure continues and is coupled with legal action, the team leader can resist erasure and test the strength of the release form, or agree to erase portions of the tape where the individual can be seen or heard.

The Network Intervention Team

My first experience as a network team member was in 1968 with Ross V. Speck as the team leader. Team members included a few therapists and often former patients who themselves had benefited from mobilizing their own network.

At a later period I made an effort to develop a more permanent team. Team members were selected from a number of professional colleagues interested in the networking process. The team included two psychologists, a psychiatrist, a social worker, a family therapist, and a drug addiction counselor, who was also responsible for video-taping the network sessions.

In working with a network team there is an ongoing need for team communication, leadership roles, development of intervention strategies, and effective teamwork.

TEAM COMMUNICATION AND LEADERSHIP ROLES

Continual communication among team members is essential. Members of my own team contributed to a training program on family network intervention. Weekly team meetings provided opportunities for team interaction, an exchange of ideas and feelings, and planning for a forthcoming network session. When referral is made for a network intervention session, a team consisting of three members should have no difficulty in attending such a session at home. When the team is larger, the team leader may need to assign a number of team members for this purpose. Team members must meet following the home visit to discuss their initial impressions, exchange their views on the nature of the family's concerns, and talk about any other concerns they may have relating to the forthcoming network session.

Effective team communication is essential among team members. The team leader may not perceive the crisis in the same way that the other team members do. The team members may frequently find themselves involved in some or all of the network phases. Team meetings can and do get stuck in a polarization phase, where sidetracking and differences of opinions are exchanged. The team can experience the mobilization and its consequent depression phases, which can last for a while before a breakthrough can occur. In our own team, there were meetings that led to effective planning and strategy development as a result of effective team communication and harmonious relationships among all members; at other times, there were conflicts because of a lack of communication and trust between the members or lack of agreement on what strategy to follow. When such conflicts develop, team members need to make every effort to communicate their differences and to resolve the interpersonal conflicts within the team.

The network intervention leader needs considerable experience and knowledge of family dynamics, group process, intervention techniques, and teamwork. Each network intervention leader may have his or her own style for leading the team. My experience suggests that there is some similarity between the leader's style in working with his or her own team and his or her preferred style of network intervention.

Some teams may decide to switch leadership roles so that each team member can experience leading the network session. Prior to any network intervention session, the team leader and the team members need to agree on fees to be paid for services rendered by each. Each team may wish to develop their own distribution system.

DEVELOPING THE TEAM'S ITERVENTION STRATEGY OF EFFECTIVE TEAMWORK

The team intervention stragegy is developed in two phases. The first phase unfolds during the team meeting following the home visit. During this meeting, the leader and the team must develop an initial strategy to mobilize the network for action. The intervention strategy that is agreed on will be based primarily on the information that the team obtained from the referral source, the discussion during the home screening visit, and the team's own impression of the dynamics of the dysfunctional relationships among the family members. The team members have to relate their impressions and offer ideas for a possible intervention approach. The team should reach a tentative strategy for the first network intervention session.

The team members' various expertise is useful at this phase. When a particular issue or dysfunctional family pattern is discussed, team members often rely on their own previous experience in dealing with similar concerns. Frequently the task demands innovations and intensive exploration of various options and courses of action to mobilize the network.

During this initial planning phase, team members are encouraged to explore in which network phase they wish to take some leadership role. Our own network team experience indicates that team members take various leadership roles during different network phases. Some team members prefer to become active during the depression phase, others in the smaller support groups that follow the sessions, and still others in meeting with the support groups between network sessions.

During the team's strategy meeting, it is best for the team leader to help team members identify their preferred areas of active involvement. These decisions are tentative; they can and do change during the actual network session.

Communication between the leader and the team is essential during the network intervention session. In our team we have found it best to agree that the leader will agree on a coleader for the sessions. The rest of the team will serve as a support team for the two coleaders. This arrangement makes it easier for the leader and coleader to involve the network rapidly during the network phases. It also allows for minimum disagreements among the team members during the sessions.

The second phase of the team strategy meeting takes place after the first network intervention session. In this phase the team should exchange impressions and experiences of the events that took place during the first network session. The team evaluates the effectiveness of the intervention techniques used, whether each of the network phases was experienced fully, in what phase the network was stuck, and why. They must take a close look at two levels, the family members and the involvement of the network. The leader and coleader then evaluate their own working relationship and the overall team functions during the session.

This second meeting includes feedback from others in the network and from the network grapevine. Team members may have had telephone contacts from the family or its friends that should be shared with the team. The team members also discuss further the impact or lack of it of the family secrets and disclosures. Team members should take a stand as to how they would deal with these secrets. Our own experience is that each situation ought to be individually considered. As stated before, it is best when the secrets can be forthcoming from the family or network members instead of from the team. However, when there are important secrets that are directly related to the crisis and that are known to the team but not to the entire network, the team has to decide how they will deal with such an issue. This decision should be based on whether the team feels the disclosure will be productive or counterproductive. If it seems productive (rarely is it not), the team may decide to expose the secret if disclosure does not come from the family members.

At the conclusion of this second team meeting, a strategy must emerge which will include each team member's role during the upcoming network intervention session, the techniques to be used, and the general direction and goals to be worked toward.

When the network intervention is completed, the team needs to meet again to discuss the outcome of the intervention session and plan for follow-up of the case. Some team members may wish to join a support group, either as temporary members or as consultants.

An important factor in the development of the team is the trust among each of the team members. When the leader and each team member feel comfortable with each other, the team can function effectively. The trust and quality of a team relationship can be obtained by continuous communication and networking among the team members. This process is time consuming, but it is an important part of a successful family network intervention process. Like families, teams can become dysfunctional in their relationships and lose their effectiveness. This may occur as a result of conflicts over leadership roles, power struggles within the team, and differences of opinion over intervention modalities. When efforts to resolve such issues do not succeed, consideration should be given by each team member to the usefulness of remaining part of the team. In our own team, after 2 years of effective teamwork, differences over leadership roles and intervention styles resulted in a decision by the team leader and the team members to seek independent opportunities for the development of their own teams with different leadership roles, directions, and team composition.

Chapter 6

TRAINING THE NETWORK
INTERVENTIONIST

Most professionals involved in helping families need to become aware of the potential usefulness of mobilizing the family social support system. A training program that tries to familiarize professionals with all aspects of the networking process must define its training goals. In our training program efforts are directed toward familiarizing professionals involved with problem families or problem groups in mental health facilities, guidance clinics, schools, correctional facilities, crisis centers, and hospitals with both the theoretical and clinical applications of family and social network intervention. To achieve this broad goal, three types of programs were developed and implemented: an introduction seminar in family and social network intervention; an advanced seminar; and continual training and consultation with the staffs of various mental health facilities on network intervention techniques and strategies of working with difficult patients and family systems.

THE INTRODUCTION SEMINAR IN FAMILY AND SOCIAL NETWORK INTERVENTION

This seminar is conducted once weekly for 10 weeks. Fifty trainees are usually selected to attend the seminar, which is offered twice a year. The primary focus during the training is given to disturbed, malfunctioning crisis-oriented family and social systems. The specific training goals for this introductory seminar are to familiarize trainees with the criteria for network referrals, the network phases, intervention techniques used during the sessions, the home visit, the theoretical framework of networks, and the practical applications of this intervention modality. To achieve these goals, the training program includes both content and experiential components that are built into the program from the first session.

Each of the weekly 3-hour training sessions is equally divided to allow trainees sufficient time to become acquainted with each other's and their own family roots and personal networking processes. Personal exploration of the trainee's own family network is encouraged, because it permits each trainee to become familiar with the potential resources available within his or her own social and family network. This experiential training component is usually preceded by videotape presentations of network intervention with crisis families, staff presentation on network intervention theory and techniques, simulated prenetwork home visits, simulated network intervention sessions, presentation by families reporting postnetwork follow-up and, whenever possible, the chance to attend a network intervention session.

EXPLORING THE TRAINEE'S FAMILY AND SOCIAL NETWORKS

The training program emphasizes active group exploration of one's own network of family and friendships. Trainees

are encouraged to prepare themselves prior to the meetings by exploring at home and activating often forgotten
family relationships and friendship systems. During the
training sessions, they meet in small support groups to
share their own findings; they focus on past and present
functional and/or dysfunctional family and friendship networks. The training emphasizes exploration of these networks as additionally useful resources and support systems
in the trainee's own life.

These trainees support groups function throughout
the 10-week training seminar. Our networking process often provides greater awareness of one's own family system
of resourcefulness, strength, or weakness. The personal
sharing continuously provides a valuable learning experience that allows trainees a greater appreciation and understanding of the process of networking families in crisis.

USING SIMULATION IN TRAINING

It is desirable that trainees observe and participate in a real
network intervention session. Whenever such a session is
forthcoming, trainees in our introductory seminar are encouraged to attend. The events that unfold during such a
session are a valuable learning experience for the therapist
who is interested in becoming familiar with the networking
process. To date, the paucity of such networks makes it
difficult to rely on them on a regular basis. We, therefore,
stress simulated home visits and network intervention sessions as the second-best training modality.

SIMULATING THE HOME VISIT

To allow trainees to become familiar with the criteria used
for selecting and referring families for network intervention, simulated home visits are developed by both staff and

trainees; this allows the trainees to play both family roles and network team roles. Family crisis roles are developed; here trainees prepare to role play family members who are experiencing a severe crisis. The home visit is undertaken by trainees role playing members of the network team, interviewing the family, discussing issues such as the nature of the problem, duration, and previous efforts made by the family members to resolve the crisis, preparing the family for the possibility of network intervention if they so decide, and making plans to help the family members prepare for mobilizing their own family and social network.

Since our training group is large, three or four such simulations are prepared by trainees in collaboration with the training staff. Following these simulated home visits, debriefing of roles is conducted by the staff. Trainees are encouraged to share their own experiences in role playing either a family or a network team member. They can question the work of the team, and the justification for mobilizing a network for each of the simulated family home visits. The family home visit that seems most closely to meet the criteria for networking their family is usually selected for a simulated network intervention session.

THE SIMULATED NETWORK INTERVENTION SESSION

All trainees are encouraged to take various roles as members of the social and family networks. The assignment of roles is done in several ways. The staff can assign roles to the trainees, or members can select their own roles in the network. When time allows, the most effective way of role playing a network intervention session is first to insure the selection of trainees to roles of members of the nuclear family. Once each family role and the crisis have been assigned, members of this family are each to contact other trainees by telephone; they assign them family and friendship roles, inform them briefly of the nature of the crisis, and invite them to attend a family network intervention session.

When the trainees meet the following week, the entire session is planned to permit the simulated network intervention process to proceed. The training staff, with the assistance of some selected trainees, acts as the network intervention team. The session is videotaped and, at the conclusion of the simulation, the trainees again are debriefed as to their feelings during the session as they played various family and network roles. In the debriefing period there is an exchange of experiences by each trainee; this is a valuable learning experience that approximates quite effectively the experiences of leading and participating in a network intervention session.

THE USE OF VIDEOTAPES IN TRAINING

Videotapes of family network intervention sessions are used regularly in the training program. The videotape presentations cover a wide variety of dysfunctional family systems during the process of network intervention. Trainees can observe network intervention sessions with suicidal and labeled "psychotic" family members, efforts to mobilize network support systems for severe marital crisis, and related difficult family crisis situations. The video presentations provide a number of valuable learning experiences. The trainees can become familiar with the variety of family crises and dysfunctions that can benefit from mobilizing the network. Trainees can see the intervention team at work and can question the usefulness and timing of specific intervention techniques used during the session.

After the video presentation, the training staff discusses and elaborates on the team's intervention goals and strategies with the trainees, and discusses the follow-up of the intervention efforts and the efforts in mobilizing effective support systems for each family member. Whenever possible, family members that do change are encouraged to return and share with the trainees their own experiences before, during, and after the network intervention sessions.

ADVANCED TRAINING SEMINAR

The goal of the advanced training seminar is to prepare trainees for active roles as network intervention leaders. Trainees selected for this program have previously attended the introductory training seminars. These advanced trainees meet biweekly; their training includes theoretical and research aspects of networking families in crisis, reviewing videotapes, participating as coleaders in network intervention sessions, and evaluating the problem families that are seen by each trainee in his or her own setting. The most difficult aspect of the advanced seminar is the low frequency of family network intervention sessions, which results in the trainees' inability to become experienced in coleading such sessions. Trainees are encouraged to develop and lead small network teams within their institutional settings where they can, under supervision, actively explore additional ways to develop social and family support systems for families in crisis.

ON-SITE CONSULTATION AND TRAINING

An on-site training format enables the staff to familiarize themselves with networking families in crisis in a practical way. Such a program should be designed so that members of the staff could adapt the network intervention process to their own specific needs. It can include videotape presentations, simulated network intervention sessions, and family screening interviews at the facility where one member of the family or the entire family are being treated. On-site consultations and training can help staff members experience the network phases. This process usually provides increased staff communication and productivity, and the development of a small network intervention team that can seek additional opportunities for applying the network concepts in their own settings.

Two recent examples of on-site consultation provide additional insights into the format and techniques of training staff with family and social network intervention. One such training was conducted by myself and Ross and Joan Speck. The team was invited to conduct a 2-day training in a psychiatric facility in Canada. During the first few hours the staff discussed with our team our experiences in conducting network intervention sessions and some of the more useful approaches of working with difficult and dysfunctional family systems. Communication between the team and the staff was done through an interpreter, since most of the staff preferred to communicate in French.

Since the French versus English issue was quite intense among the staff, the team suggested a network intervention simulation with this issue as the main concern. A roleplaying situation was selected by the hospital staff in which two professional married staff members working at the same hospital have marital difficulties stemming, in part, from disagreements over which school their 8-year-old daughter should attend, an English- or French-speaking one. The husband role played an American psychologist, his wife was French speaking, and their views on the subject were diametrically opposed. Polarization occurred rapidly among the staff, after a team member suggested that the discussion should be focused on the feminist versus racist points of view.

The simulated experience was followed by the staff members joining a number of support groups that continued their efforts in providing options for the couple. This simulated experience also gave the staff a firsthand chance to experience the network intervention process.

On the second day, videotape presentations were observed. The team provided one such presentation, while staff members showed their videotaped efforts of a network intervention session with a French-speaking family. This on-site training allowed both our team and the staff of the psychiatric hospital to exchange useful information. This on-site visit could encourage the staff to explore other opportunities for applying the networking concepts in their own setting.

In a more recent consultation, the staff of a psychiatric facility was interested in exploring the feasibility of mobilizing the social and family networks for a family of seven, whose members were patients in the facility on several different occasions. Several staff members who saw some of the children individually while they were hospitalized reported that religious differences among the two parents and the children's separation from home were traumatic experiences for the entire family system. The family was briefed on the possible usefulness of networking their system, and they agreed to come for a screening interview, which was to be attended by 15 staff members. The team for this consultation consisted of myself, my wife Mira, and Ross and Joan Speck.

A 1-day training was designed. During the morning and early afternoon, a videotape was presented; it was followed by a discussion with the staff on the methodology of network intervention. Later in the day an interview was conducted with the family. The team planned this screening interview to be similar to a regular network intervention meeting. The rationale for this type of format was that it allowed both family members and the staff to experience a "taste" of the networking process before deciding whether or not to mobilize the entire system.

When the staff sought permission to videotape the

session, the father agreed, provided that his oldest daughter's boyfriend would not attend. Following some arguments between this daughter and her father, the entire family entered the room. Both parents were in their late fifties, and the children's ages ranged from 12 to 23.

After a brief retribalization consisting of milling around, Indian whooping, and singing, the polarization phase rapidly developed. The team tried to learn whose side the children were on. With the exception of the youngest child, who preferred to sit next to his father, the children chose a neutral position, backing away from both parents. The father and mother remained sitting at opposite sides of the room. Both parents were adamant that their point of view was the correct one. A mobilization was experienced when each child was asked to reunite the parents temporarily by sitting next to each other, eyes closed, telling both parents what they needed from them. A depression phase followed when the youngest son broke down and began sobbing; he pleaded with his parents to stop fighting and express more love and caring.

At the conclusion of this brief session, which lasted for less than an hour, the staff and the family formed a circle and hugged each other tightly. The team shared their impressions with both the family and the staff. Family members sought clarification as to the process of inviting other network members. The final decision about mobilizing their network was left for the family members to decide after discussing it at home.

The team members were able to let the staff observe some of the networking techniques used, and provided them with a new option in dealing with the family in a different fashion. Both the staff and the team felt that networking the family system could provide the involvement of other significant people in this family's life who would be able to provide support for each family member, search for crisis resolution, and decrease the likelihood of dependency on hospitalization.

Chapter 7

FAMILY NETWORKING
INTERVENTION TECHNIQUES

There are a number of techniques that help members of the intervention team to mobilize the family network toward its goal of crisis resolution. Some of these techniques have been used previously by other practitioners in individual and group settings, primarily during encounter, Gestalt, psychodrama, and family therapy sessions. These techniques can be used during the network intervention sessions to achieve specific goals for each of the network phases. The techniques are grouped into three categories: retribalization, polarization, and mobilization.

RETRIBALIZATION TECHNIQUES

This series of techniques can produce an increased level of participation, rapidly involving the network members in a sequence of verbal and nonverbal activity that usually is experienced as fun; it helps members to increase their energy levels, thus contributing toward an effective retribalization phase.

During the milling around activities, network members have a brief period during which they can introduce themselves to others and share some initial impressions and information. These activities are designed to involve the network in an initial expenditure of physical energy that is needed if the network is to become retribalized effectively. Network members often report feeling "childish" or "stupid" while engaged in these activities. Few members object to becoming involved during this phase.

The team leader must allow any network member who chooses not to become engaged in an activity the option of doing so. Some members remain uninvolved and join the activity later; others select one activity and avoid another. The leader and the team usually participate in these activities while also allowing for questions or clarifying the need for a specific activity during this phase of the network intervention session.

Network Milling

As the network members assemble, they are instructed to mill around and make contact with as many people in the room as they possibly can during a 3-minute period. They greet each other, exchange bits of information, and move on to meet someone else.

A number of variations can be helpful. Members are instructed to regulate their speed of milling around so that all can mill slowly; then they mill around at a faster rate. While doing this, members can be instructed to shake hands, slightly touch each other's backs, shoulders, heads, or legs. They can bump lightly as they mill around at a faster or slower rate, and they can talk, hum, or be completely silent during the milling activities.

Network Screaming/Whooping/Clapping

To release the network's energy level further, members are asked to scream simultaneously, then pair up, exchange first names with their partners, and scream each other's first names. Variations include simultaneous screaming and jumping up and down in place, or small groups screaming each other's names. Another variation is whooping Indian style, followed by hand clapping and foot stamping.

Circle Movements

The network members form a circle, hold each other's hands, and move toward and then away from each other as one body, without disengaging their hands. Variations include developing a sound that represents their collaborative efforts, moving toward different directions, or forming concentric circles and repeating the movements and sounds.

The Family Song

Members of the nuclear family are asked to suggest a favorite melody. The entire network then joins in singing this melody. A number of variations exist. The network members sing the melody while clapping hands, swaying, or both; they sing the melody loudly or hum it softly; or they sing a medly of songs that are suggested by various network members.

The Network Speech

The team leader introduces himself or herself and the team, and briefly outlines the need to work toward solving the family's problems; he or she indicates that there is a crisis and that the team needs all the help it can get from the network in helping the family to solve the crisis. The leader emphasizes involvement, sharing, openness, and the development of support. He or she defines the main role of the team members, who function as helpers in the process of healing the family. The emphasis is on active involvement with the concerns of the family.

The Network News Time

When there is more than one network session, the team encourages members of the nuclear family, the support groups, and other network participants to take a few minutes and share with the network the events that occurred during the past week. The team leader shares what he or she has heard through the network grapevine, and encourages others to do the same.

The network news time is basically a form for initiating communication and information that should be shared by the entire network membership. It can be a source of validation and confirmation of events that occurred between network sessions. It could also be a way of correcting misinterpreted communication and feedback.

POLARIZATION TECHNIQUES

These techniques are used frequently during the polarization phase. Their use allows for rapid involvement by members of the family with their extended social support system. The polarization phase often occurs without much utilization of such techniques. However, the use of these techniques is needed when the network has difficulty in becoming actively involved in the networking process, because this results in little polarization.

The Inner-Outer Network Circle

Members of the nuclear family are requested to sit in an inner circle and make brief statements about the conflicts as they perceive them; an outer circle forms behind them. Following the completion of the family member comments, members sitting in the outer circle switch places so that they are now sitting in the inner circle, while members of the nuclear family are in the outer circle. Network members in the inner circle are asked to comment, to share their thoughts and feelings about the statements made by the nuclear family.

The Empty Chair

An empty chair is placed in the inner circle. A network member who wishes to comment takes a seat in this empty chair, makes a statement, and then vacates the chair.

A modified version of this could consist of the team leader saying to the network member: "Sit next to the one you feel closest to"; "Sit next to the one you can trust"; or "Sit next to your friend."

"Whose Side Do You Take?"

This more provocative statement is often used to help network members examine their own statements and motivations. Two responses are typical, a neutral one or a confirmation that the individual sides with a specific family member.

Variations include, "Whose side are you on?" and "Who do you support?" When people are able to confirm their support for one family member, they can be asked to sit next to that family member.

Another variation is to ask, "Who is having a problem in the family?" "Is there only one problem?" "Are there any secrets in the family?" These statements can stimulate further discussions and encourage a greater level of exploration by the network membership.

Removing a Family Member

When the network's energies are focused toward one family member to the exclusion of others for a length of time with little significant progress attained, the possibility of a scapegoating process increases. To stop this process, the team leader has a number of options available. He or she can state his or her observation to the entire network, suggest a change in the topic for discussion, or suggest that other family members should be involved in the process. When these interventions do not produce significant changes, the leader can ask the individual who is the center of the network's attention to step to the back of the room or, if necessary, temporarily leave the room, accompanied by a team member.

When the scapegoating process is quite severe, members will often leave the room without being told to do so. They should not be stopped from leaving since, in almost all cases, their absence shifts the focus of the network's attention to a more intensive exploration of the events that led to the family member's departure. A member who has left the room usually returns to the session after a brief "cooling off" period, because he or she cannot resist involvement with the network.

Communicating with an Absent Member

When an important member of the family is unavailable due to sickness, an unwillingness to attend, or a death in the immediate family, the leader must encourage one or more family members to communicate their feelings toward this absent member, particularly when he or she is part of the emotional dysfunction and crisis. The therapist can arrange for the family member to speak to the absent member by having the family member imagine the absent member sitting in the empty chair. Other family and network members can be of help in this dialog by carrying on a conversation with the absent member.

Another way to achieve this goal is to encourage a network member who is familiar with the family's concerns to take the role of the absent member and continue the dialog. A dialog with an absent member can often be done by calling the absent member on the telephone and discussing specific issues of concern.

During one network session, the family dog was the network messenger, carrying messages from the members back and forth from the first to the second floor, where one family member was hiding and refusing to participate physically with the remainder of the network.

MOBILIZATION TECHNIQUES

The use of these techniques can help the network members to mobilize their resources effectively, particularly during the mobilization and depression phases. Their use should be timed to achieve a specific result. Most of the techniques promote direct confrontations; this often results in strong and cathartic expressions of emotions that lead toward effective and productive networking efforts by the social and family support systems.

Promoting Direct Confrontations

During each network session there are several occasions when family members must confront each other directly. Their inability to do so often slows the network process and prevents successful crisis resolutions. The team leader can use a number of techniques to help family members express their feelings effectively.

One such technique is to ask a family member to step up onto a chair and talk to the family member he or she wishes to confront. Several variations are possible. As one member stands on the chair in an elevated position, the other kneels down and looks upward. The member on the chair is instructed to speak loudly or even scream at the one he or she wishes to confront. A number of family and network members can be helpful by standing on both sides of the chair and giving additional support for the confronting member. The family member on the chair and the confronted member may wish to switch places so that the one on the floor now stands on the chair.

Another variation is to ask both members to stand apart, look into each other's eyes and, without speaking, walk toward each other, expressing nonverbally any feelings that they wish to express. There are many options; some familiar ones are to proceed and hug each other, turn their backs on each other, push each other away, or stand at a distance unable or unwilling to move.

The team leader frequently must become involved in helping a reluctant and passive member to confront another member directly. The team leader can support the member by physically embracing the member from behind while encouraging him or her to speak directly, completing statements such as "I wish . . . ," "I need . . . ," "I desire . . . ," and repeating these statements several times with increased vocal intensity.

The outcome of these family confrontations can provide a number of responses, ranging from anger, hurt, and disappointment to tenderness, love, and affection. As the feelings are expressed, the issues become clearer and give the network members further opportunities to become involved in a helpful and supportive manner.

Simulating Disengagement from Home

At times the team leader needs to help family members experience and acknowledge that leaving home, at least temporarily, is a feasible and desirable alternative. There are a number of techniques available to involve the family and the network in achieving this goal. One such technique is "breaking in-out of the circle." It requires that the network members form a tight circle, holding to each other's arms, while the family member inside the circle is asked to break out of it physically. A reverse procedure is also possible and involves having the family member break into the circle from outside it. This breaking out of the circle (or into it) can represent a symbolic disengagement from home and can help to mobilize further the entire network for additional action.

Another disengagement technique is the "rope technique." The team leader ties a rope to the waist of one family member and attaches the other end to the waist of another family member. As an example, a rope is tied around the waist of an older son and around the waist of his mother. The two are then told by the team leader that that is how he or she views their relationship. They are connected to each other and, in the leader's opinion, the relationship is destructive. Either one is asked what his or her intentions are with regard to this relationship. This situation usually provokes others in the network to comment on the relationship and also give suggestions for changing it. Whatever the outcome of this experience, it can and does provide much discussion as to the options available and the need for change in the relationship.

The "Death Ceremony"

A powerful technique for dealing with issues of disengagement as well as loss of a family member is the "death ceremony." The family member selected by the team leader for this experience is asked to sit on a chair or lie on the floor and imagine that he or she is dead. The person is covered with a sheet, and members of the family are then requested to eulogize the member's death. The team leader encourages each member to kneel beside the "dead" family member and express his or her feelings. Anyone in the network may pay final respects to the "dead" person. Following this experience, time should be made available for network members to share their feelings and experiences. This technique usually stimulates the experiences and feelings related to issues of past death and loss in the family, such as feelings of mourning toward one's own parents, spouse, or offspring.

Sculpturing the Family Network

Specific crisis situations that may be a contributive factor to the crisis in the family can often be worked through by the development of various family and network sculpturing techniques. One such technique requires the family members to arrange themselves spatially to depict a particular feeling they have toward one another. Each family member may wish to change another member's spatial position if they feel it presents a more accurate representation of the events occurring at home. Significant other extended family members may wish to place themselves as they see themselves or as others in the family view them vis à vis the crisis.

Role Playing

Family and network members can role play specific crisis situations, each choosing a role that he or she may wish to take. Following a brief vignette depicting the events that took place, the network can contribute to a discussion and follow up on the experience with comments and feedback.

Role Reversal

Family members are assigned the roles of other family members. This role reversal provides a valuable experience of the feelings and issues with which other family and network members are struggling.

Chapter 8

TRANSCRIPTION OF THE GROSS FAMILY NETWORK[1]

(First Session)

THE FAMILY

Jerry Gross: 27 years old, twice hospitalized for la-
beled "psychotic" episodes and suicidal attempts
Gertrude Gross: Jerry's mother, in her late fifties
Linda Gross: Jerry's 20-year-old sister

THE SOCIAL NETWORK

Bill: Jerry's friend
Dora: Mother's sister
Dorothy: Mother's sister
Eileen: Cousin
Henry: Cousin

[1]This case was discussed in Chapter 2.

Jim:	Jerry's cousin
Nina:	Father's sister
Nora:	Neighbor
Rita:	Cousin
Riva:	Jerry's cousin
Rona:	Jerry's cousin
Saul:	Jerry's uncle
Sarah:	A mother who was helped previously by assembling a network for her family
Simon:	A neighbor

THE INTERVENTION TEAM

Uri Rueveni, Ph.D.: Team leader

Muriel Wiener, M. S. W. and S. J. Marks, M.F.A.: Team coleaders

Bernice Tucker, Ed.D. and Geraldine Spark, A.C.S.W.: Family therapists who previously worked on the case

The people in this network were invited by Mrs. Gross, her son, Jerry, and her daughter, Linda. They have been in family therapy with little reported progress. Jerry has been hospitalized a number of times for "bizarre behavior" and frequent suicide attempts. Since his father died a few years earlier, Jerry's affective depression and strong symbiotic bond to his mother have been difficult problems to correct. His sister Linda felt depressed, quit school, and stayed at home. The goals of intervention were to mobilize the Gross' extended system of family, relatives, and friends who could provide the needed push for both mother's and son's separation, and for the development of a support system for all three family members.

The first session took place in a hospital videotape facility on a Sunday afternoon. There were 50 people in attendance, including family, relatives, friends, and family therapy students. I introduced myself and my team. I asked the participants to identify themselves and indicate their relationship to the Gross family.

When this task was completed, I proceeded with the network speech.

Uri: I am sure that the Gross family is thankful for your willingness to come and help them today. What we are trying to do is quite difficult and we need all of you to participate actively in helping the Gross family help themselves. As a team we are relying on all of you to listen and act. We will have two network sessions and we do hope that by the time we end today there will be enough people who become involved with the family by telephone calls, offers of ideas, and help with their concerns so that, as a result, the Gross family can say, "We can do something with our lives." (This initial charge is intended to prepare the network for the events to come.)

I continued to retribalize the network by a sequence of structured experiences designed to increase the network's energy level.

Uri (continues):   We usually begin each network by some physical activity that helps all of us increase our involvement and level of energy and readiness to participate. Will you please stand up? Now, let us all jump up and down in place and scream as we do so. Now, please pair up with an individual who is near you, exchange your first names, and then jump up and down and scream each other's names.

This activity creates an increased energy flow, and reduces the initial tension and uneasiness felt by many in the network.

I then asked the family to lead the network in singing their favorite melody. Someone began to hum the melody

"Sunrise-Sunset" from *Fiddler on the Roof* as the group stood in a circle, first humming, then singing the melody. Mrs. Gross suddenly began sobbing. She was hugged by her sister as the network members continued to sing the melody.

When the singing was completed, the three family members sat in a circle in the middle of the room surrounded by their relatives, while the other network members took their seats in chairs and on the floor.

Uri: I would like to ask you, Jerry, to begin by sharing with us, from your point of view, the problem that exists in your family.

Jerry: Well, I guess I'm living at home and am dependent on my mother and right now I am not working. (Remains silent.)

Uri: You have got about 70 seconds more to go.

Jerry (smiles):   It's difficult at home. I'm a little apprehensive about looking for a job, and I don't know what to say.

Uri: How about you, Linda?

Linda: Well, there's a lot of friction at home. Everybody wants to get their way and it interferes in what other people want. For example, if my mother wants the house to be clean and my brother wants to lay around and watch TV, it interferes with him. If I want to do my work and for it to be quiet and it's not quiet, or if he wants dinner or something and he wants me to cook and I don't feel like it. Well, you know, there are a lot of things like that.

Uri: Yes, Linda. What's his problem? (Points to Jerry.)

Linda: I guess he has nothing to do with himself. (She then remains silent.)

Uri: Mom, what's the problem?

Mrs. G. (begins to sob as she talks, looking toward her son):   I work very hard and when I come home at night he

wants me to feed him and if I don't feed him he pushes
me and shoves me. I can't take any more. (Continues
sobbing.) I try to pay all the bills. I do everything. I
don't feel well. (Looks quite helpless as she sobs, raises
both hands upward.) And he doesn't offer to go to
work or anything. He thinks everything is coming to
him. I am the slave. I have to clean up while he takes
the pillow upstairs and the pillow downstairs. He
watches TV, turns the air-conditioner off and on.
When my husband was sick he bought the air-conditioner in the dining room for his health. I fight with
him (Jerry) each time he turns the air-conditioner on.
I have to pay the bill. I just can't take it. When I come
home I want to first eat my dinner and he says, "First
you wait on me" and if I don't, he takes the coffee and
spills it on me.
As she continued, I stood up and asked the family members
to sit next to Mrs. Gross and her children.

Uri (talks to small group just assembled):   What can you
    make out of it? You discuss this among yourselves.
Dorothy (Mrs. Gross' sister):   Well! I will start. I talk to my
    sister every day, maybe four times a day. She has had
    a very, very, very hard life through marriage, through
    childbearing. She lost one child. Her husband died. He
    wasn't too wonderful, but he worked! In fact, he died
    working! While driving a cab. (Continues to speak very
    determinedly, pointing a finger toward the group as
    she talks.) She has tried to make a living for her two
    children. She (points to Linda) has been to college and
    he (points to Jerry) has been to college. He has been
    to law school because that is what he wanted to do and
    this little lady (points again to her sister) has tried her
    darndest. She would fund their education and would
    let them go on and on but at this point (points again
    toward Jerry) all she asked of him was to get work, any

kind of work. Physical work, anything, not even pertaining to mental work. He doesn't have to be a lawyer,
doesn't have to be an accountant! Nothing to tax his
brain. Just a job. This is the family. (Points in a circle
to other people assembled around her.) There isn't
one person here who doesn't work for a living. Not
one. Not one! But this young man (points again toward
Jerry) doesn't want to look for a job and has a fear of
the outside world. And if somebody is kind enough to
try to put him in a job, he doesn't hold it! Something
goes wrong.

Muriel: Has anybody in the family tried to help?

Dorothy: Yes!

Uri (speaks to Dorothy):   Would you repeat what you just
said, Dorothy, but speak directly to Jerry?

Dorothy (looks at Jerry):   Whenever somebody was kind
enough to put you in a job, Jerry, it didn't last. I wasn't
there to find out what went wrong. Am I right or
wrong? (Jerry nods his head affirmatively.)

Saul: I have a restaurant and I tried to get Jerry to help
me and I offered to pay him something and he went
there and after a couple of hours he said, "I just can't
do it." Is that right, Jerry? (Jerry nods his head affirmatively.) You felt you just weren't fit for it. You were
tired; your feet hurt. Is that right? I tried to help you.

Henry: My wife tried to get you a job at the store.

Jerry: Yes! That was good.

Henry: So why did you quit?

Mrs. G.:   He got sick! He got sick! He had to go to the
hospital for 6 months.

Nina: He doesn't want to work. First he said he couldn't
see. He said it was the medication.

Uri: Talk to him directly.

Nina: Jerry, am I right? You said you couldn't see. You
couldn't go look for a job. You couldn't see the print
in the paper to even look for an application for a job.

Then you said you could see and that you wanted to go places but lacked ambition to go places. You don't want to go out of the house. You just want to lay.

Mrs. G.:   Yes! He told me to look for a job for him.

Nina: Yes! She was always the one. He always wanted his mother to find a job for him. He wanted to be a substitute teacher. His mother had to make the calls for him.

Jerry (screams):   I don't like this. I'm sorry. (Stands up, angrily leaves the room.)

Mrs. G.:   Sit down. Sit down, Jerry! (She tries to go after him and the network members raise their voices, "Leave him alone. Let him go.")

Uri: Let us continue. He is finally honest with himself. When he wants to come back, he will. His spirit is still with us!

Dorothy: That is right. Let's continue because they don't know the true story (talking to Nina).

Nina: The true story is that Jerry wants his mother to do everything for him. He doesn't want to make any effort. None whatsoever!

Eileen (Jerry's cousin):   I don't know how I would feel if I had a problem and if everyone told me to my face, and everyone is sitting here and listening to all my failures. I don't know how I would take it.

Dorothy: May I answer this, Eileen, because you hardly ever get in touch with the family (talking to Eileen). Do you realize that this is almost the end of the road? Do you realize how many times Jerry was in hospitals? Do you realize anything?

Eileen: I am only making a statement and I am asking the doctor.

Dorothy: And I am trying to answer you.

Uri: I don't think I would like to answer this question. This is your network.

Eileen: I can understand that, but if I was Jerry, I would be upset, too. That is how I feel and everyone's entitled to his feelings.

Dorothy: Excuse me, Eileen. Have you heard about professional psychiatry? You're an educated girl. You are a schoolteacher. Jerry has been involved in individual therapy and group therapy, but this is something entirely different because we are all desperate. You are not aware of that.

Eileen: I understand that. You told me on the way over here how desperate you all are, and I am not putting any of this down.

Dorothy: So, what are you trying to say?

Eileen: I'm just feeling for Jerry when everyone is sitting around and pointing a finger at him.

This frank exchange of conflicting feelings is critical for the unfolding of the polarization phase now in progress. To encourage greater involvement, my team and I used the "empty chair technique."

Uri: Let's ask the people who are sitting on the outside of the circle to comment. Please tell us what you feel is going on. (Takes a chair and puts it next to Mrs. Gross.) Anybody who has a comment, please come to the chair and let us know how you feel.

Jim: Jerry has always felt that people were hostile to him, and I don't think that hostile attitudes in this family are going to help Jerry. He has made a lot of mistakes, and he has always been reprimanded severely. His father was very, very tough on him. And I think being punished severely for each mistake he has made has brought him to the point where when he sees something and it is tough for him to face, he runs away immediately. We are not going to achieve anything at all if we are going to keep up this hostile attitude. I don't think we have to take his mother's side or blame Jerry, because this will only keep him away from us.

Uri: Good comment! How about some other people?

Rita: I was just going to say the same thing. I cannot see any sense in putting Jerry down, since everything he has tried failed. And maybe that is why he spends all of his time in his room and that he is up all night and sleeps all day, just so that he doesn't get near people. But not one person yet has said what he could do to help him.

Saul: We were told to say that to him and that is the reason that we said it. (Looks at me.) Maybe we shouldn't have.

Rita: O.K.! It's not the idea of why you said it but exploring why Jerry feels this way.

Saul: You ask him. He won't answer you.

Rona (Jerry's cousin):   In discussions with Jerry, everybody talks to him and they talk to him and he doesn't offer any comment or any answer. I am not around him very much of the time, but I can talk to him about little things. When you ask him about himself, what's he done, or what's he going to do, he doesn't respond back. I think all of us in the family know this, and I don't think anyone in this family wants to hurt his feelings.

Uri (talks to Sara, whose daughter was involved in a previous network intervention session):   Do you have any comments to make? (Sara takes a seat in the inner circle.)

Sarah: My name is Sarah. (As she begins talking, Jerry returns to his seat in the middle of the room.) My family has had a network. I have a daughter, 32, who was in the network, and I am a widow. Jerry, all of this is very wonderful. It's all part of a scheme to make your family better.

Uri: Come on, Sarah. Tell us what you really feel.

Sarah: I feel that Jerry cannot help what he does. If he could, he wouldn't be ill. Now you can pounce on him until you are blue in the face. You can criticize him, whip him, even feel like killing him. It won't help. What he can use is your help, all of you people. You want this family to be better. My daughter has changed a great deal since her network and now, for the first time in my life, I am free to be myself. I am not bound by this terrible thing of having to take care of her. That is what threatened me, too.

Dorothy: I think you are a wonderful person, Sarah. We are all trying desperately to have Jerry do something some place away from his mother. Not even pertaining to physical work.

Sarah: Yes. Maybe he needs someone away from the family.

As the conversation continued, I talked to some of the men.

Uri: I would like to have some of the men in this room, those who feel like helping Jerry, sit around him and continue to discuss in what way Jerry can use them as resources.

A group of men assembled around Jerry and shared with him their feelings regarding various issues such as his previous work habits and his off-and-on pattern of finding a job and then quitting; they were trying to understand and appreciate what goes on at home when he is not working and consider the possibilities of helping him in his struggles. As the group continued to discuss the various issues around Jerry's problems, two other groups slowly began to assemble, one group around Mrs. Gross and another group around Linda. The three groups continued discussions for about 30 minutes and produced constructive discussions, but not with sufficient energy and involvement to break the impasse. The network seemed "stuck" in a depression phase. The team planned its next strategy. Muriel Wiener took the role of a family choreographer in an attempt to develop a family sculpting with the three members. This permitted additional group efforts at moving the network out of the depression phase.

Muriel: Mrs. Gross, Jerry, Linda, would you please stand in the middle of the room. (Mrs. Gross stands close to her son and Linda stands across from them.) This is your family. Linda, I want you to take your mother and brother and place yourself as you feel yourself in this situation right now. How do you see yourself in this family?

Linda: Right where I am now.

Muriel: On the outside?

Linda: Yes.

Muriel: You mean they are together?

Linda: Yes.

Muriel: What do they do? What are they doing as you are looking at them from the outside? Take their hands and show them how you want them to stand.

Linda: They are together.

Muriel: Why?

Linda: Because they always are.

Muriel: So there are always fights—physical ones and words. (Linda shakes her head affirmatively.)

Muriel: What do you do when the fights go on? Do you just stand there?

Linda: Yes! Either that or I walk away because there's nothing I can do.

Muriel (asks Linda to position herself physically between her mother and brother):   Don't you feel like this sometimes? (Tells mother and brother to push and squeeze her.) Does that feel like that? Lean against her, Mrs. Gross, because you need her, don't you?

Mrs. G.:   Yes!

Muriel: Jerry, do you need your sister?

Jerry: Yes!

Muriel: So lean on her, too! (Now Linda stands sand-

wiched between her mother and brother.) How does it
feel to be between those two?

Linda: Not too good!

Muriel: Is that what it feels like? What does it feel like to
you?

Linda: I want to leave this and get out.

Muriel: You can't.

Linda: Why?

Muriel: Because there is weight on you and also because
you love them and you need them. What are you going
to do?

Linda: I can't push Jerry away because he's too big.

Muriel?   Try it. Push him.

Uri: Push him.

Muriel: Push him.

Linda: I can't.

Muriel: Are you afraid of what will happen?

Linda: Yes. He is going to punch me.

Uri (talks first to Muriel and then to the entire group):
How about if we have volunteers to stand up around
Linda and create a circle, preventing Linda from getting out of the circle? Linda, your task will be to force
yourself out of the circle. (A group of 15 network members assemble around Linda, including her mother and
her brother, as Linda struggles to force her way out of
the circle. Linda fights her way out as the network
members encourage her to try harder and get out. For
about 3 minutes the group prevents Linda from breaking out, until finally she is able to push her way out.
The entire group claps their hands and cheers her for
being able to do so. She softly sobs and a friend hugs
her warmly. Another circle forms. This time Jerry is
asked to stand inside the circle and push his way out
of it. Jerry pushes as the group members in the circle
attempt to prevent him from leaving. He finally suc-

ceeds in bursting out of the circle, and the network members congratulate him for his efforts.)

As a follow-up of the sculpting experience, Jerry and his sister fighting their way out of the circle could represent a symbolic disengagement from home. The experience involved additional efforts by many more network members, giving them their first chance for direct involvement. The team strategy developed now; it was aimed at capturing this increased involvement by the network in allowing both son and mother to begin a separation process. The "funeral ceremony" was chosen as the most effective strategy in achieving this goal.

Uri (instructs Jerry to lie on the floor, face up. Takes a sheet and places it over Jerry's body. Then turns to Mrs. Gross, who sits on a chair next to her son, and asks her to kneel beside her son):   Mrs. Gross, Jerry is dead. He is not home anymore. How do you feel?

Mrs. G.:   Let him be on his own.

Uri: Talk directly to him.

Mrs. G.:   Right! I want to live my own life. It's time already. I did everything I could for you. It's time you started to live alone. It's time for you to live your own life.

Uri: Talk to him.

Mrs. G.:   I am past 60 and it's time for me to live my own life and not have the responsibility of cleaning for you, doing for you. It's time you should go out and work and be on your own and I would be very happy. I want to live my own life.

Network member: Do you have a boyfriend?

Mrs. G.:   I had a boyfriend, but he has given me up because of my son.

Network member: Tell him that.

Mrs. G.:   He knows it. My boyfriend says that if Jerry straightens up, then there may be a chance, but until then he wants no part of it.

Uri (to Linda):   How do you feel about your brother being dead?

Linda: I just wished you would have been successful instead of laying around and ruining my life.

Muriel: What else?

Linda: That's all.

Uri: Anyone who would like to come and express feelings toward Jerry, please do so.

Mrs. G. (begins to sob):   All my life I worked and worked, let him go to college so he should be a success and prayed and prayed. (Sobs loudly.) My father on his dying bed said, "Wait. That boy's going to be great when he grows up." Instead, what does he give me? Torture and misery. He pushes me around and shoves me and says, "Do this for me and do that for me" like I am just a slave. Oh, God Almighty! (Continues sobbing.)

Uri (picks up another white sheet and covers her, too):   I would like the family to come. Each of you come and tell the three of them what goes on inside of you.

Mrs. G.:   My heart is broken. (Continues sobbing.) I want to live my own life. I am getting older and I want to live my own life.

Saul: Jerry, if you don't straighten up, you are going to lose your whole family. You won't have anybody. You will be by yourself.

Jeff M.:   Tell him what you are feeling.

Saul (leans down and takes Linda's hand as he continues talking to Jerry):   I will try my best to help you, but you have to help yourself first. You have to show me that you are willing and able to do something for yourself. I will continue to help you.

Cousin: Jerry, I would like to be just proud of you and think that you should be helpful to yourself as well as to your mother and sister and you went to school and a lot of people had a lot of hard times getting jobs and trying to continue their efforts.

Muriel (cuts in in the middle of the sentence):   Tell him what you are going to do for him.

Cousin: I would like to help him if I could.

Jeff M.:   Tell him how you are going to do it.

Cousin: I could always be there if you needed someone to talk to. I don't think I could find you a job. If I could, I would.

Uri: Good. (To the network.) Continue your comments! Please come over and express your feelings.

Dorothy: I like him. I always did like him. I will always like him.

Rita (kneels down and takes Jerry's hand):   Jerry, this is Cousin Rita. Right now I know you hate me, but you remember when you left the psychiatric hospital and you came to my apartment and you sat there and you trusted. . . .

Jeff M. (interrupts):   Tell him what you feel right now.

Bernice: Tell him what you are going to do for him right now.

Rita: Whenever you knocked on my door, I answered. We sat in the bedroom. I brought you food. I will bring you food.

Bernice (to Rita):   Say, "I want you to come!"

Rita: I want you to come (as she leaves to return to her seat).

Jim: Jerry, you know you can always come to me. We can talk on the phone for hours. We can do it again. You can always turn to me.

Jeff M.:   Tell him what you want.

Jim: I want you to come and talk to me. I want you to try to understand me. To try to understand what you want to do because you can have anything you want.

Jeff M.:   Tell him whether you like him or not.

Jim: I like you. I'm always willing to spend time with you. Anytime! Anytime you feel like it.

Uri: Good! Who's next?

Terry (a neighbor):   Jerry, I am Terry, your next-door

neighbor. Come over to my house and have a cup of coffee like we did a couple of months ago.

Rona (leans over beside Jerry, sobbing):   Jerry, it's Rona. I have been away for a long, long time, but I only live two blocks away from you. Come visit and talk with me. We all love you.

Uri: O.K. Anybody else?

Nina (her voice cracks as she begins talking and holding Jerry's hand):   Jerry, I want to be your friend. I always cared about you.

Uri: (Pulls the sheet off Jerry's body. Asks Jerry to share his feelings.)

Muriel (to Jerry):   Does it make you feel uncomfortable that you are the center of all this?

Jerry: Yes. I feel people care about me, but I still don't care about myself.

Uri (to Mrs. Gross):   You want all the people here to give your son a job.

Mrs. G.:   No! But some suggestions so that he could go to work. He just lies around on the sofa.

Uri: What do you want for yourself? How can we help you?

Mrs. G.:   Just that I should live on my own. I work every day very hard. I am very conscientious. I want to get married, if I get a boyfriend. I don't go out to the movies or dinner.

Muriel: I want to know from you people what you are going to do.

Jim: I will tell you exactly what I will do. I am more than happy to take him (Jerry) in and show him what I do. Teaching him how to work. But he's got to want it for himself.

Gerry S.:   What time are you going to pick him up this week?

Jim: On Tuesday.

Muriel: Good, because we are going to ask for a report during this time.

Gerry S.:   What happens after Tuesday? Does anyone have any time for Jerry?

Simon: Monday he could come with me.

Muriel: Is anyone in this network prepared to help him have fun?

Bill: Saturday morning I will pick you up to go fishing. (Approval is voiced by many in the network for this commitment.)

Uri: I would like to hear Mrs. Gross, Jerry, and Linda share with us briefly their feelings at the end of this session.

Mrs. G.:   I feel much better. I felt lonely when I came in. I feel more encouraged now. There are friends and family who do care.

Bernice: She has arisen! (Takes Mrs. Gross' hands and lifts them.)

Gerry S.:   Everybody is in the process of being reborn!

Mrs. G.:   It is not all solved yet, but I am more hopeful today than ever before.

Uri: Jerry, how about you?

Jerry: I feel people care a lot, but I still feel attacked.

Linda: This experience is weird. I cannot believe all this is happening. It is really an overwhelming experience.

Saul: Linda, that is right. It is difficult, but that is why the family is here. We do care.

Uri: We have to end now. Please remember to exchange telephone numbers and meet with your support group this week. We will see all of you next week for the second session.

As the first network came to an end, the support group members formed around Jerry, Linda, and Mrs. Gross, making plans for their next meeting.

Chapter 9

ADAPTATION AND APPLICATIONS
OF THE NETWORKING PROCESS

Can professionals and others who are involved in helping families in a host of agencies, hospitals, clinics, schools, and related community organizations modify, adapt, and use the concepts of social networks? Can the energies, resources, and commitments that are available within the social network become a productive and supportive force to be used in a variety of settings? Can we, as Sarason (1977) has challenged, "bring people together so that by exchanging resources they can generate new ideas, energies, possibilities and capabilities"? This chapter attempts to provide an affirmative response. The concept of a network as a supportive system is indeed a challenging one. It is based on interconnectedness and on increased reliance of people working toward some common goals. If one can conceptualize the network as Sarason did, as "a resource locating and resource matching vehicle for helping people alter perceptions about resources and relationships, reduce feelings of isolation, frustration and routine" then the possibilities for adapting the networking process are numerous.

In recent years a growing number of formal and informal network support systems have developed, aimed at helping people with a host of difficult problems, including rape, runaways, and child, wife, and drug abuse, to partake of services and programs for marriage and family enrichment. One common thread in most of these networks is the use of the social network for support and the exchange of resources available. This chapter describes different ways of utilizing the concept of network as a supportive system. Hopefully these ideas and others developed by the readers can be adapted and utilized in different settings.

MOBILIZING PARTIAL FAMILY NETWORKS AS A SOCIAL SUPPORT STRUCTURE FOR HOSPITALIZED PATIENTS

The social network can be utilized to help deal with a developing crisis experienced by psychiatric patients during their stays in such facilities. For some patients disrupting news from home, a family member, or a close friend can be contributing to the development of such a crisis. For others, an anticipated discharge from the facility may provoke extreme anxiety and a relapse of symptoms. Staff efforts can be directed toward the development of additional support for these patients. The reconnection of the supportive structures with the patient can provide the staff an opportunity to utilize additional resources available in the family, friendship, and community system. As reported earlier, Garrison's work in convening partial networks during admissions and throughout the hospitalization phase, and Callan's et al. use of the social network in helping drug-dependent residents prior to re-entry to the community are two examples of the use of the social support system in an inpatient facility.

There is often little interest or motivation by the family to engage further in helping a hospitalized member. When efforts at reconnecting the family with their ailing member for increased participation are nonproductive, consideration can be given to convening the staff and other community resources in providing the additional energies and efforts needed for crisis resolution.

In a recent case, a 14-year-old boy who was court-committed to the facility had had numerous crises with his parents, staff, and the law. Two events triggered consideration for convening a partial network. One was his request for a weekend outside the facility; the other was his upcoming discharge. The staff was concerned about an unsupervised weekend. The feeling was that the risk was too great to let the patient leave the facility on his own. Another concern was the patient's request to return home after discharge from the hospital, a request that was denied by his parents.

The initial networking efforts were to assemble the staff working in the unit and some community "activists," some of whom knew the patient, since he had sought their services (drug abuse, runaway). I led the meeting; the main aim was to network the staff, who were seeking alternatives and options of first dealing with the weekend issue and, second, finding prospects for mobilizing support for the young man upon discharge. One staff member volunteered his home for the patient to stay in during the weekend. Another offered to take the patient and her own son, who was the same age, to a local zoo and to a movie. Considerations were also given to contacting the parents, meeting with them, and discussing the ways in which they could mobilize their own support and that of others in their system who would be willing to help the young man live a more productive, less destructive, life.

A similar intervention approach can be used in a psychiatric inpatient facility that offers educational and therapeutic programs to disturbed adolescents. One such format can include all staff that are directly involved with the hospitalized adolescent; these staff members can attend a number of family sessions where the networking process increases appreciation by the family members of the needs, problems, or lack of them, of their adolescent son or daughter. Such meetings are attended by all family members and the entire staff of the unit that is involved in the treatment and educational aspects of the patient. Such networking could be led by an outside consultant or by an assigned staff team, whoever is the most familiar with the concerns of the family and their hospitalized member.

Another format within such a setting can include mobilizing the family and staff around a developing crisis with a hospitalized member. Such a crisis may be a lack of involvement in school, refusal to cooperate, aggressive outbursts toward staff or toward a fellow patient, or a suicide attempt. The networking process may take place during a regular staff meeting and can include small support groups that offer the parents and others in the family additional help in dealing with their crisis.

The networking process basically involves the hospitalized family member, the immediate family, and the staff in a session aimed at changing the crisis by providing an ongoing process of involvement in which the available support group discusses options for crisis resolutions. This networking process may be particularly helpful to the family when their ailing member is about to be discharged. When family members are unable to maintain adequate supervision or support, a network session that includes other family members, relatives, and friends can be arranged, either in the hospital setting or at home, to develop a temporary support system for the entire family.

This networking process can be utilized with a variety of patients in a number of hospital, clinic, or correctional settings where the social support system needs to be mobilized in a crisis during treatment or for support after discharge to the home or the community.

MOBILIZING SUPPORT FOR SUICIDAL MEMBERS

Another variation of the networking process could take place at the point where a phone call from someone threatening to take his or her own life comes in to one of the many suicide prevention centers. When contact can be established with the caller and the family, an intervention team can, if feasible and with permission, visit the caller. Arrangements can proceed to "reconnect" the person with any available family and relatives for an initial meeting to discuss the concerns at hand. Contact with previous professionals who may be familiar with the individual will be helpful in developing intervention strategies that may, if appropriate, include a family network intervention session or a modified network where options can be considered in helping the individual.

The call may originate from a distraught parent to a mental health emergency room or a mental health professional. The mobilization of a supportive group of people around the crisis does not preclude other therapeutic efforts that need to be taken into consideration. Instead, these efforts can be viewed as complementary aiming toward the development of a social support system that, if mobilized effectively, can provide many opportunities for the development of constructive options.

PROBLEM-SOLVING STAFF CONCERNS

Experience with a variety of staff problems, primarily in mental health settings, indicates that one of the more promising approaches to solving staff crises could involve a modified networking process. A major part of any staff problems that lead toward crisis proportions in any organization are interpersonal in nature. Lack of communication between staff and management could contribute toward the development of negative attitudes, lack of morale, absenteeism, and low motivation. Staff development programs that recognize the similarity between the problems that develop within the family system and those that occur in work settings succeed in their efforts to change attitudes. Positive changes in staff can occur for many reasons, however, and one of the best methods of insuring effective staff functioning is staff networking.

Especially when a crisis develops among the staff that hinders proper daily functioning, consideration should be given to setting aside time for the entire staff and management in an attempt to explore the issues and develop an ongoing communication mechanism that will enable a greater familiarity among staff members and allow them to appreciate the various needs, expectations, and goals that each one has about their service with the organization. Often a network intervention session can result in providing the staff with its own support system, which can function more cohesively and productively.

THE USE OF NETWORKS IN COMMUNITY CRISIS

Recent years have evidenced a proliferation of social network support groups for rape, child and wife abuse, gang intervention, and drugs, all in an attempt to fill the gap of needed community and social services. Most community-type crisis can benefit from the establishment of a networking support system to solve a crisis. The form of such a networking process can vary from one type of crisis to another. For example, in a recent effort to deal with the spreading drug use in a housing project near the psychiatric facility in which I work, an attempt was made to mobilize all community resources, including all families living in the project, their children, their friends, and members of the social agencies that provided help to this project. The networking process tried to establish a base for the development of support groups to give families whose members were already using drugs a place to turn.

Some support groups were dealing with the issue of increased violence in the project, others with individual cases of family crisis, and still others with arranging for the purchase or donation of recreation equipment for the children and adults living in the project. Arrangements were also made to provide some psychiatric consultation at the nearby psychiatric facility, and for an ongoing consultation related to crisis resolution in the project.

In another part of town, a group of street blocks organized themselves into a network of 50 members; in their weekly meetings with the neighbors they considered issues such as how to deal with the increasing incidents of rape in the neighborhood. The group developed a network support system that provided free medical, psychological, and financial help to any rape victim living in the neighborhood. Their continuous efforts at networking their own community is another excellent example of how the networking process can be adapted for constructive use in developing options that could help in dealing with community crisis.

NETWORKING PARENTS AND THE FAMILIES OF MENTALLY HANDICAPPED CHILDREN

Most treatment and school facilities engaged in working with mentally handicapped children and youth attempt to provide a variety of supportive services that can help the child and his or her family utilize the educational and therapeutic experiences that the staff can offer.

In many such facilities the therapist functions as a member of the treatment team. Members of such teams are usually skilled and experienced with various aspects of providing the care needed for treating and/or educating these special children. The administration of these facilities should encourage the treatment team's members to develop additional intervention modalities that include, if possible, therapeutic services to families and the ongoing networking of these families as a supportive structure.

The example selected here is based on my experience as an informal consultant to one such team member, a family therapist who initiated a series of supportive services to families and the staff in a nonresidential school for retarded children.

I believe that although differences do exist between such a facility and those that serve essentially disruptive children or youthful offenders, with modification, such a program could be adopted and be helpful.

One of the main concerns of the team was the lack of motivation on the part of some parents to become involved as a family unit in working through difficult crises, marital and familial frictions, and often dysfunctional relationships that affected not only the emotional lives of their special child but other children in the family.

Prior to consulting the family therapist, the school team made efforts at meeting some of those concerns by bringing in periodic consultants and outside "experts" to consult with the staff (and often with the parents) on a variety of issues. They discussed the child's retardation, family problems, and a host of related issues. Although these efforts were educational, they were insufficient to energize or mobilize the parents' motivation to become more involved in problem-solving efforts and in mutual resource exchange.

In consultation with members of the team (the social worker, nurse, and vocational coordinator), the school principal, the administration, and some of the teaching staff, the therapist developed therapeutic and educational intervention models that included family therapy to families whose children attend school, parents' groups, staff development, and a parents' support network.

Since family therapy was a voluntary service, the motivation to join this opportunity was not initially high. The impetus for family problem-solving involvement came only after parents' participation in weekly "parenting groups," which were content-oriented group discussions on topics related to effective parenting, a "mothers' group," which allowed "time out" for the mothers of special children to share their concerns, and a "couples' group," where couples discussed issues that affected their relationship as a couple with a special child.

As trust developed between these group members, the therapist and other team members' requests for involving the entire family became much more frequent. As these efforts progressed several in-house staff development workshops were developed for the teaching staff to allow increased awareness to, and familiarity with, the work of the therapist and the therapeutic team efforts in developing an integrated plan for parents' involvement with the school and with each other. These workshops included themes such as communication, problem solving, and family systems intervention.

THE PARENTS' SUPPORT NETWORK

This program provided a unique opportunity for the parents of special children to utilize the resources of the school staff and of each other. Up to that point, parents who brought their young children for the "early stimulation program" had little opportunity to interact with each other or mobilize their own or each other's resources.

The program consisted of 40 parents, all new to the

school, who were requested to leave their children for treatment in the school for one half day each week on a Saturday morning while they were given various lectures on topics related to their child's problems. Although these were important topics, parents had little time for interpersonal exchanges, and the utilization of the supportive resources gained from meeting together as one group. The initial design, which allowed the parents to meet once every 6 weeks with the family therapist for a brief period of time, was a format that prevented effective networking efforts.

After consultations with the school team and the administration, the therapist proposed that priority be given to networking the parents' resources for support and for a greater school-parent collaboration. The rationale for this change was: (1) to give the parents a better chance to exchange their feelings on specific issues relating to their parenting roles; (2) to develop a more cohesive support group; (3) to allow the parents "time out" for sharing their needs and expectations from the school and from each other; (4) to provide a forum where the efforts can be directed at increasing the parents' involvement with the school's concerns and utilizing the parents' energies to develop additional ideas for the school-parent collaboration; and (5) to develop an ongoing parents' resource and support network that would provide a vibrant link between the school and the community.

To help the therapist in her efforts, a small group of parental group leaders was trained. These paraprofessional leaders assisted the therapist as group leaders. The leaders were supervised weekly and served as important "network activists" in this continual effort to mobilize the parents' resources.

The first year of the program evidenced a marked increase in both parents' and school's participation and efforts. This network process is continuing, with the parents' support group leading the way at reconnecting with additional sources of support such as reaching out to other parents, getting increasingly involved with school projects and, most significantly, relying less on the therapist as the crucial link and relying more on each other.

SOME NATURAL USES OF FAMILY NETWORKS

Mobilizing the family tribe has been a continual life process. Various cultures and ethnic groups assemble their family networks for religious and traditional functions. Many families today have much more difficulty in getting together, especially if they are separated geographically and emotionally. Family celebrations and funerals are common events at which most of the available family network meet for a brief period of time.

The process that occurs during these natural events is similar to the networking process during crisis. One major exception is the lack of intentional mobilization or team intervention. The family networking process occurs within a natural and often expected set of events. The opportunity for increased intensity and involvement with the natural web of family network is obvious. However, not many families are willing to take advantage of such an opportunity to examine their relationships, which would provide a new opportunity to heal old wounds and make new commitments for change. Perhaps the difficulty lies in the family members' unwillingness to admit mistakes and to save face, avoid embarrassment, and deny family concerns in an attempt to preserve the "good" family name. The difficulty in networking the family without outside help may be an additional factor. Whatever the reasons, there is still room and need for the networking of the family system during such natural and predictable family events. Each family may wish to innovate in developing their own pace of self-examination, aiming toward increased communication, contacts, future collaborations, and reunions.

FAMILY NETWORK INTERVENTION: SUMMARY OF PHASES, TASKS, AND GOALS

Appendix 1 Family Network Intervention: Summary of Phases, Tasks, and Goals

Phases	Tasks of Family & Network	Tasks of Intervention Team	Goals
Retribalization	Family calls together network members and provides setting for meetings	Explain rationale and significance of network meeting Reduce tension through encounter-type exercises	Make network visible Begin rebuilding ties between network members
Polarization	Family presents to network problems/issues creating crisis Network members present different reactions to the issues	Have subgroups of the network present, uninterrupted, their views and feelings about problems	Draw out different attitudes and feelings of members Promote confrontations that shake up old stereotypes and lead to new interpersonal perceptions
Mobilization	The entire network or (smaller groups), work to generate possible solutions to specific problems	Present specific problems to network Facilitate group interactions, discourage unproductive communication	Focus energy and resources of network on creating new solutions to problems

Appendix 1   Continued

Phases	Tasks of Family & Network	Tasks of Intervention Team	Goals
Depression	Network members get discouraged, frustrated with difficulty of task	Acknowledge difficulty and provide encouragement Use psychodramatic techniques helping the network break the impasse	Regenerate positive feelings of solidarity and support to offset feelings of discouragement Help network keep working on difficult task
Breakthrough	"Activists" generage workable solutions	Mobilize support structures for each family member Promote effective small group interaction	Provide new solutions to problems
Elation/exhaustion	Potential solutions developed, new feelings of satisfaction and competence fill group. Future connections are planned	Encourage support group members to plan course of action	Feelings of satisfaction and competence centered in network, reinforcing value of network meeting

This chart is modified from an original version prepared by Marc Goldstein.

THE FUNCTIONS OF THE TEMPORARY SUPPORT GROUP MEMBERS

During the Network Session	*Between Network Meetings*	*Following the Completion of the Network*
Network "activists" take clear positions by supporting one or more family members	Support group members meet with the family member to plan an initial course of action and begin to develop alternative options in solving the crisis	Support group members continue to meet and help the family member they chose to support reconnect with additional sources of support from each of them and/or others in the family and community
Network "activists" are encouraged by team members to initiate and lead the way in efforts to organize and form support groups	Support group members maintain telephone contact with each other, the family, and the team	Resources are pooled to tap available social contacts, jobs, housing, and related community contacts
Team members encourage the formation of support groups for each member of the nuclear family unit	Support group members attempt to develop and mobilize resources and plan ongoing as well as future strategies for support	Contact is maintained with family and team members through face-to-face meetings, phone calls, and letters
		Support group members attempt to develop additional goals that may meet their own needs in participating as effective members in such a group

Appendix 3

FAMILY AND SOCIAL NETWORK INTERVENTION

Training Course Outline

This is an introductory 10-week course. We will meet on 10 consecutive Friday afternoons from 1 to 4 P.M. Please try to attend all seminars, since the course material is designed with your participation in mind. The course includes weekly discussions on specific topics, followed by a video-tape presentation or a lecture-demonstration that is related to that topic.

SEPTEMBER 30:
SYSTEM INTERVENTION AS AN EVOLVING NETWORKING PROCESS

1. We will explore each other's interests, expectations, needs, and experiences or lack of them. Our aim today, as it will be during the following 9 seminars, is to allow our own networking process to evolve, thus experiencing the network bonding by actually becoming involved in it.

2. We will also be looking at dysfunctional family relationships that lean toward crisis, stagnation, and non-productiveness by selecting a number of family vignettes that depict a family crisis and role-playing them. After a discussion of these cases, we will select one family vignette to be expanded and developed into a full crisis in need of possible network intervention. The concept and rationale for utilizing the network approach will be discussed following the vignettes.

OCTOBER 7:
THE PROCESS OF HELPING A FAMILY MOBILIZE ITS SOCIAL NETWORK FOR ACTION

1. A previously selected "family" unit will be interviewed for possible consideration of mobilizing their own as well as their social and extended network resource for help in solving the family's crisis. Following the role played family interview, a discussion will highlight the criteria used in selecting a family for this modality of intervention, the need for teamwork, the development of strategy, and the help given to the family members in utilizing the opportunity to reconnect with their extended system.
2. Mobilizing the network's support system during a marital and family crisis.
Videotape presentation and discussion of case.

OCTOBER 14:
MOBILIZING THE NETWORK SUPPORT SYSTEM—A SIMULATION

1. We will attempt to help a "family in crisis" reconnect with its extended system of relatives, friends, and neighbors in a search for additional sources of strength and support, and to develop alternatives for solving the family's

ongoing crisis. The simulation will be videotaped and led by the instructor and a selected team of family intervention-ists.

2.   We will process the simulation and discuss the events that did and did not take place.

OCTOBER 21:
THERAPISTS' INTERVENTION STYLES WITH FAMILIES AND THE EXTENDED SYSTEM

1.   We will explore our own as well as other styles of intervention with families.

NETWORK INTERVENTION WITH A DEPRESSED WOMAN AND HER FAMILY SYSTEM

2.   Videotape presentation of mobilizing support for a depressed woman, her husband, and their two children. A discussion of the case will follow.

OCTOBER 28:
THE THERAPISTS AND ISSUES OF FAMILY MEMBERS' SEPARATION AND DISENGAGEMENT

1.   We will explore issues of productive and nonpro-ductive separation from home, family, spouse, and/or friends.

THE SOCIAL NETWORK AS A SUPPORTIVE STRUCTURE FOR PRODUCTIVE DISENGAGEMENT

2.   A videotape presentation depicting the process of helping a 14-year-old girl and her family modify their dys-

functional relationship by a process of disengagement and separation, leading toward a more productive family functioning.

NOVEMBER 4:
THE THERAPISTS' WORK WITH "PSYCHOTICS" AND THEIR FAMILY SYSTEMS

1.   We will discuss our experiences and knowledge of working with labeled "psychotic" family members.

NETWORK INTERVENTION—AN EFFECTIVE APPROACH IN MODIFYING SELF-DESTRUCTIVE SYMBIOTIC BONDS

2.   A videotape presentation of efforts made to mobilize the social and family support systems' attempt to help mother and her "psychotic" son cut their mutual self-destructive cord.

NOVEMBER 11:
THERAPISTS' APPROACH TO SUICIDE AND DEATH

1.   We will share our feelings and thoughts regarding suicide, death, and the mourning process.

NETWORK INTERVENTION WITH A SUICIDAL FAMILY MEMBER

2.   A videotape presentation of the process of networking the extended family system to stop a suicidal pattern will be shown.
A discussion and follow-up of the case will be shared.

NOVEMBER 18:
THERAPISTS' WORK WITH DRUG-ABUSING FAMILY MEMBERS

1.   We will discuss the issue of the use and abuse of drugs and exchange views, experiences, and strategies to include the family system in the helping process.

NETWORK INTERVENTION WITH A DRUG-ABUSING FAMILY MEMBER

2.   A videotape will demonstrate the process of mobilizing the family system to help its drug-abusing member.

NOVEMBER 25:
OUR NETWORKING EFFORTS

1.   We will examine our progress or lack of it in our networking efforts to date and consider issues that were not as yet clarified or discussed.
A simulation, videotape, or additional discussions will follow, depending on the issues brought up by the group.

DECEMBER 2:

1.   An examination of the various roles we undertake while working with the family and its extended system.

References

Allisi, A. S. Social work with families in group-service agencies: An overview. *Family Coordinator,* 1969, **18,** 391–401.

Attneave, C. L. Y'all come: Social networks as a unit of intervention. In P. Guerin (Ed.), *Family therapy: Theory and practice.* New York: Gardner Press, 1976.

Attneave, C. L. Therapy in tribal settings and urban network intervention. *Family Process,* 1969, **8,** 192–210.

Auerswald, E. H. Interdisciplinary versus ecological approach. *Family Process,* 1965, **7,** 202–215.

Barnes, J. Class and committees in a Norwegian Island parish, Human Relations 1954, 7.

Bell, N. W. Extended family relations of disturbed and well families. *Family Process,* 1962, **1,** 175–193.

Bleisner, J. A community model of networking in family networks and beyond. *Journal of Alternative Service,* 1976, **2,** 28–29.

Boissevain, J. *Friends of friends: Networks, manipulators and coalitions.* New York: St. Martin's Press, 1974.

Boszormenyi-Nagy, I., & Spark, G. M. *Invisible loyalties.* Hagerstown, Md.: Harper & Row, 1973.

Bott, E. *Family and social network: roles, norm and external relationships in ordinary urban families.* Travistook Publications, London, 1957. New York: Free Press. 1971.

Bowen, M. Towards the differentiation of self in one's own family of origin. In F. D. Andres (Ed.), *Georgetown Family Symposium: A Collection of Selected Papers*, 1971–1972, Vol. 1, pp. 77–95.

Brown, V. Community crisis intervention: The dangers of and opportunities for change. In H. Parad, H.L.P. Resnick, & L. Parad (Eds.), *A mental health sourcebook*. Springfield, Ill.: Charles C. Thomas Co., 1976, 99–105.

Callan, D., Garrison, J., & Zerger, F. Working with the families and social networks of drug abusers. *Journal of Psychedelic Drugs*, January–March 1975, **7**, 19–25.

Caplan, G. *Support systems and community mental health*. New York: Behavioral Publications, 1974.

Caplan, G., & Killilea, M. *Support systems and mutual help*. New York: Grune & Stratton, 1975.

Cohen, R. Post-disaster mobilization of crisis intervention teams: The Managua experience. In H. Parad, H.L.P. Resnick, & L. Parad (Eds.), *A mental health sourcebook*. Springfield, Ill.: Charles C. Thomas Co., 1976, 375–383.

Curtis, W. R. Community human service networks, new roles for mental health workers. *Psychiatric Annals*, 1973, **3** (7), 23–42.

Erickson, G., Rachlis, R., & Tobin, M., Combined family therapy and service network intervention. *Social Worker*, Winter 1974, (Canada) **41**, 276–283.

Erickson, G. D. The concept of personal network in clinical practice. *Family Process*, 1975, **14** (4), 487–496.

Feldman, F., & Schertz, F. *Family social welfare*. New York: Atherton, 1967.

Foxman, J. The mobile psychiatric emergency team. In H. Parad, H.L.P. Resnick, & L. Parad (Eds.), *A mental health sourcebook*. Springfield, Ill.: Charles C. Thomas Co., 1976, 35–43.

Garrison, J. Network techniques: Case studies in the screening-linking-planning conference method. *Family Process*, 1974, **13**, 337–353.

Garrison, J. Working with the families and social networks of drug abusers. *Journal of Psychedelic Drugs*, January–March 1975, **7** (1), 19–25.

Garrison, J. Network methods for clinical problems. In E.M. Pattison (Ed.), *Clinical group methods for larger social systems*. Symposium presented at the 31st Annual Conference of the AGPA, February 1976, Boston, Mass.

Garrison, J. Community mental health nursing: A social network approach. *Journal of Psychiatric Nursing and Mental Health Services*, January 1977, 32–36.

Garrison, J. A network approach to clinical social work. *Clinical Social Work Journal*, 1977, **5** (2).

Garrison, J. Community intervention with the elderly: A social network approach. *Journal of the American Geriatrics Society*, 1976, **24** (7), 329–333.

Guerin, P. (Ed.) *Family therapy: Theory and practice.* New York: Gardner Press, 1976.

Haley, C. The contemporary need for intentional networks. *Journal of Alternative Services*, 1976, **2**, 25–26.

Hammer, M. Influence of small social networks on factors in mental hospital admissions. *Human Organization*, 1963, **22**, 243–251.

Hansell, N. Patient predicament and clinical service as systems. *Archives of General Psychiatry*. 1967, **14**, 204–210.

Hansell, N. Reception service in emergency contexts: Facilitating adaptational work. In H. Parad, H.L.P. Resnick, & L. Parad (Eds.), *A mental health sourcebook.* Springfield, Ill.: Charles C. Thomas Co., 1976, 15–23.

Jones, M. *Beyond the therapeutic community: Social learning and social psychiatry.* New Haven, Conn.: Yale University Press, 1968.

Katz, R. The painful ecstasy of healing. *Psychology Today*, 1976, **10**, 81–96.

Kleiner, R. J., & Parker, S. Network participation and psychosocial impairment in an urban environment. NIMH Grant MH 19897, Final Report, 1974.

Kliman, A. The Corning flood project: Psychological first aid following a natural disaster. In H. Parad, H.L.P. Resnick, & L. Parad (Eds.), *A mental health sourcebook.* Springfield, Ill.: Charles C. Thomas Co., 1976, 325–334.

Langsley, D., & Yarvis, R. Crisis intervention prevents hospitalization. In H. Parad, H.L.P. Resnick, & L. Parad (Eds.), *A mental health sourcebook.* Springfield, Ill.: Charles C. Thomas Co., 1976, 25–27.

McGree, R., & Heffron, E. The role of crisis intervention services in disaster recovery. In H. Parad, H.L.P. Resnick, & L. Parad (Eds.), *A mental health sourcebook.* Springifeld, Ill.: Charles C. Thomas Co., 1976, 309–320.

Minuchin, S. *Families and family therapy.* Cambridge, Mass.: Harvard University Press, 1974.

Papp, P. Family choreography. In P. Guerin (Ed.) *Family therapy theory and practice.* New York: Gardner Press, 1976.

Pattison, E. M. Social system psychotherapy. *American Journal of Psychotherapy*, 1973, **17**, 396–409.

Pattison, E. M. Psychosocial system therapy. In R. G. Hirsh & B. Levy (Eds.), *The changing mental health scene.* New York: Spectrum, 1976.

Pattison, E. M. (Ed.) Clinical group methods for larger social systems. Symposium presented at 31st Annual Conference of the AGPA, February 1976, Boston, Mass.

Rueveni, U. Family network intervention: healing families in crisis. *Intellect,* May–June 1976, 580–582.

Rueveni, U. Network intervention with a family crisis. *Family Process,* 1975, **14,** 193–204.

Rueveni, U., & Speck, R. V. Using encounter groups techniques in the treatment of the social network of the schizophrenic. *International Journal of Group Psychotherapy,* 1969, **19,** 495–500.

Rueveni, U., & Wiener, M. Network intervention of disturbed families: The key role of network activists. *Psychotherapy: Theory Research and Practice,* December 1976, **13,** 173–176.

Rueveni, U. Family network intervention: mobilizing support for families in crisis. International Journal of Family Counseling, 1977, **5,** 77–83.

Sarason, S. B., Carroll, C. F., Moton, K., Cohen, S., & Lorentz, E. *Human services and resource networks.* San Francisco: Jossey-Bass Co., 1977.

Satir, V., Stachowiak, J., & Taschman, H. *Helping families to change.* New York: Aronson, 1975.

Selkin, J., & Braucht, N. Home treatment of suicidal persons in emergency and disaster management. In H. Parad, H.L.P. Resnick, & L. Parad (Eds.), *A mental health sourcebook.* Springfield, Ill.: Charles C. Thomas Co., 1976.

Speck, R. V. Family therapy in the home. *Journal of Marriage and Family Living,* 1964, **26,** 72–76.

Speck, R. V. Psychotherapy of the social network of a schizophrenic family. *Family Process,* 1967, **6,** 208–214.

Speck, R. V., & Attneave, C. *Family networks.* New York: Vintage Books, 1973.

Speck, R. V., & Rueveni, U. Network therapy—A developing concept. *Family Process,* 1969, **8,** 182–191.

Speck, R. V., & Rueveni, U. Treating the family in time of crisis. In Jules Masserman (Ed.), *Current psychiatric therapies,* (1977 edition), **17,** 135–142.

Tolsdorf, C. C. Social networks, support, and coping: An exploratory study. *Family Process,* 1976, **15** (4), 407–417.

Zuk, G. *Process and practice in family therapy.* Haverford, Penna.: Psychiatry and Behavioral Science Books, 1975.

INDEX